College and Society

An Introduction to the Sociological Imagination

Stephen Sweet
Cornell University

Allyn and Bacon

Boston ■ London ■ Toronto ■ Sydney ■ Tokyo ■ Singapore

Senior Editor: *Jeff Lasser*
Editor in Chief, Social Sciences: *Karen Hanson*
Editorial Assistant: *Susan Hutchinson*
Marketing Manager: *Jude Hall*
Manufacturing Buyer: *Suzanne Lareau*
Cover Administrator: *Kristina Mose-Libon*
Electronic Composition: *Omegatype Typography, Inc.*

ISBN: 0-205-30556-3

Printed in the United States of America

10 9 8 7 6 5 4 3 2 1   05 04 03 02 01 00

To Jai, Arjun, and Nisha

CONTENTS

ACKNOWLEDGMENTS

A number of people contributed effort and insight to *College and Society*. Special thanks to those who offered criticism of early drafts, including Jeffrey Chin, LeMoyne College; Margaret Lowe, Bridgewater State College; Donna Dempster-McClain, Cornell University; John Massaro, SUNY-Potsdam; Phyllis Moen, Cornell University; Robert Orrange, SUNY-Oneonta; and Steven Ward, Western Connecticut State University. Jackie Rush, and Akshay Gupta offered expert help in the fine-tuning of the manuscript. Karen Hanson and Jeff Lasser of Allyn & Bacon proved to be wonderful editors. Thanks also to my students, who read, listened, and responded to my early attempts to bridge the gap between college and society.

The Journal of College Student Development generously allowed me to revise my article "Understanding Fraternity Hazing: Insights from Symbolic Interactionist Theory" for Chapter 2. Appreciation is also extended to the Alfred P. Sloan foundation (Sloan FDN #96-6-9 and #99-6-3; Phyllis Moen–Principal Investigator), for support of the analysis of academic careers presented in Chapter 3.

Finally, a special debt of gratitude is owed to Frank McLaughlin, who first introduced me to the discipline of sociology, as well as to the ways of connecting sociology to personal experience.

Stephen Sweet

1 College, Society, and the Sociological Imagination

Academia is commonly referred to as "the ivory tower," the place where scholars and students stow themselves away to wrestle with abstract ideas. It stands in marked contrast to "the real world," the place where people concern themselves with things that are of practical importance. But are colleges and society as removed from one another as the ivory tower metaphor suggests? One wonders whether life in a university is unique, or whether it reflects the ways in which society normally operates.

The closer one looks at the patterns of interaction in colleges and universities, the structures that confront students and faculty, the culturally based expectations of social conduct, and the historical trajectories of university life, the more one appreciates how similar academia is to the society existing beyond its confines. In the chapters that follow, I pose college and society as mirror reflections of each other, examining the characteristics of one in the reflections of the other. Although each chapter stands independent of the other chapters, all share a common theme suggesting that what transpires in college society reflects the social processes occurring in the wider society. Conversely, what sociologists already know about the operations of society can be used to understand the workings of colleges and universities.

This first chapter offers a brief introduction to sociology, the discipline that I use to frame the subsequent studies of college and society. Unlike its sister discipline, psychology, which attempts to explain human conduct in terms of variations in individual capacities or traits, the sociological imagination focuses on the social relationships that surround individuals. Unlike its near cousin, economics, most sociologists see cost-benefit analysis as only a partial explanation of human conduct. And unlike the biological scientists, we are reluctant to reduce social behavior to genetic programming and survival-of-the-fittest explanations. This is not to discount the insights offered by psychologists, economists, or biologists, who have offered important discoveries about people and social behavior. However, until these observations are linked with sociological perspectives, they remain, at best, partial explanations of the human experience. What exactly is a sociological way of understanding society and how can it be used to understand the workings of colleges and universities?

The Sociological Imagination

In 1959, C. Wright Mills published *The Sociological Imagination*, a book that helped teach a generation to think sociologically. Few others have been as adept as Mills in diagnosing problems within the profession of sociology or have offered such a clearly stated advocacy for the expansion of sociological analysis to problems confronting individuals in society.

Mills argued that people such as you and I experience many personal troubles, but, without a sociological imagination, we are unlikely to fully come to terms with the causes of these troubles. For example, as I sit here writing, many of my students are cramming for their introduction to sociology class final exam. They are sweating over five chapters of reading assignments and weeks of lectures, the content of which I condensed into 75 multiple choice questions. Unfortunately, I was not able to cover all this material sufficiently during the last week of class because of time constraints, so some students are now struggling with these assignments with little guidance. An exam such as this is a personal trouble. Some students will pass and experience joy, others will fail and experience varying levels of angst. Students who fail can seek solutions in a number of different directions. Some will conclude that they are to blame and that they should have studied harder. Others might conclude that they lack the innate ability to learn the material. Others may conclude that I am simply a bad teacher. A personal trouble such as this can be resolved by finding fault within one's self or within others, and in some circumstances this is appropriate. Mills suggested, however, that if this is as far as the analysis goes, much is missed.

It is possible to reflect on my students' experiences in a different way by considering the circumstances that bring us together as teacher and student. I will frankly admit that I am not particularly happy with my use of multiple choice tests. I think that these tests are designed to assess students' ability to recall what has been read or discussed, but are not especially adept at discerning their ability to think sociologically or problem solve (concerns that have much more interest to me). This being said, why are multiple choice tests so popular and why do I use them? In the case of tenured and tenure-track professors, it may have to do with the knowledge that deans and colleagues tend to accord more importance to other scholarly activities, such as writing journal articles, than to student evaluations of courses (Marchant & Newman 1994). In the case of the ever growing pool of adjunct faculty, it may be because they are stretched so thin trying to earn a living (sometimes working at multiple colleges) that they simply lack the time to grade essay exams. One thing seems clear: multiple choice exams are used not because they are especially good at evaluating learning, but because they mesh well with the demands of modern society, which stresses speed and quantifiable results, often at the expense of quality (Ritzer 1996).

Another personal trouble confronting my students is that some of my assigned readings have not been covered during class time, which was limited to fifty minutes, three times a week, for fifteen weeks. Oddly, the encounters between students and professors in college society are not determined by how much learning is expected to be accomplished; they are determined by the amount of time they are expected to spend together. According to the social historian E. P. Thompson (1967), this is a comparatively recent innovation in the ways in which human encounters are regulated.

In historical terms, most work has not been regulated by the clock. Instead, it was guided according to the tasks that needed to be done. Consider, for instance, work on traditional farms. No matter what the conditions, when cows need to be milked or crops need to be harvested, farmers labor until the work is done, regardless of how long it takes. Thompson called this approach to work **task-oriented labor,** the normative expectation that one works at a job until he or she has accomplished the undertaking. Under this system, once the job is completed, relaxation can commence. In contrast, **time-oriented labor** is regulated by the clock, where work is measured by the amount of time workers spend laboring at a task. Time-oriented labor developed in response to the structure of an industrializing society, which needed workers to labor in shifts on the factory floor in order to keep machinery operating. Under this new system of regulating labor, workers and bosses restructured job expectations in accordance with how long a laborer works, irrespective of how much has been (or needs to be) accomplished. Paying employees by the hour, for example, does not specify how much is to be done, it only specifies how long workers should be occupied in an endeavor. In American society, this approach proved so effective at regulating production in factories that it was adopted by educators, who used factories as a model of how to structure the interaction of teachers and students (Marshall and Tucker 1992). Thus, some of the personal troubles confronting my students can be traced to events that occurred two centuries ago during the Industrial Revolution.

Thinking of an even more fundamental issue, why are students in my classes in the first place? In 1940, only one in twenty (5.9%) young adults aged 25 to 29 years old had completed four or more years of college. By 1998, one in four (27.5%) had completed four or more years of college (U.S. Census Bureau 1999). If I were teaching a century ago, my classes would not have consisted of students from working-class and lower-middle-class backgrounds but rather from more wealthy family backgrounds. Fewer still would have been ethnic minorities or women. These demographic shifts represent fundamental changes in society, including the need for an educated workforce, an expansion in the opportunities for higher education through the availability of student loans, and the repeal of some discriminatory policies on campus.

These observations highlight Mills' assertion that understanding personal problems must be linked with larger structural, cultural, and historical events. Mills posited that the trained sociological imagination concentrates on three overarching questions:

1. *What is the structure and culture of society as a whole?* **Culture** is an encompassing term that refers to everything learned and used by members of a society. This includes technology, language, customs, norms, and values. **Structure** refers to the organization and relation between components in society. This includes government, economy, educational systems, health care systems, and all other organizations functioning within the social system.
2. *Where does this society stand in human history?* Societies change and these transformations can have a profound impact on experience. To evaluate the strengths and weaknesses in the current social order requires understanding what society was like a year ago, decade ago, and a century ago.
3. *What types of people tend to prevail in society?* Success is rarely an accident, and there are multitudes of factors that influence which individuals are likely to achieve the greatest amounts of privilege. Understanding power in society requires studying politics, class systems, and the mechanisms by which social status is conferred.

The sociological imagination is not just an academic pastime, it is a vital tool that can enhance the lives of individuals and society as a whole. On one level, sociological understandings can be used strategically by individuals to advance their interests. For instance, studying future employment opportunities (a structural issue) can be used as a means to select a college major. Understanding that the desire for consumer goods is not a universal value, and that personal financial debts limit life chances, can influence one's relationships with credit card companies (Rizter 1996; Schor 1998). Knowing that images presented on television shows bear only slight resemblance to the ways in which people actually live can provide a more realistic means of appraising the level of one's own successes (Coontz 1992; Gergen 1991).

The sociological imagination can also be used to direct social change. If citizens are sociologically informed, they are in a stronger position to produce changes to society that can have a lasting impact. For example, rather than blaming national problems on self-serving politicians, a social movement for campaign finance reform could have a profound impact on how government leaders are elected. Likewise, students who suffer in crowded lecture halls, taught by underpaid and overworked adjunct faculty, may be empowered by knowing how to identify the root sources of these problems.

In some circumstances, it is more difficult to change society or even one's circumstances in that society. In these instances, the sociological imagination can be a useful means of at least placing one's personal troubles accurately within the mix of social relationships common to one's peers at this particular moment in history. Unlike the legions of self-help books that have become so popular in the past three decades, Mills suggested that less attention be focused on what is wrong with individuals and more attention be paid to our common experiences and the sociohistorical forces that shape our joys and miseries.

Drawing upon Mills's advocacy for sociology being an active and vital force, and his assertion that personal troubles often stem from public issues, the chapters that follow tend to focus on the social problems occurring in society and academia. This is not intended to imply that society is nothing but trouble, or that university life is dysfunctional. However, by identifying problematic aspects of colleges and the wider society, sociology has its greatest potential of facilitating positive change.

Sociology and Individualism

One of the challenges sociologists face is teaching people to think in terms of social relationships rather than in terms of individual people. As early as 1836, Alexis de Tocqueville (1836/1969) identified a deep-seated individualistic orientation to American culture. This orientation disposes people to understand society as being little more than an accumulation of separate individuals (Bellah et al. 1985). Because society is understood primarily in terms of individuals in isolation from one another, Americans tend to look for explanations of social behavior by looking for faults or strengths in people, rather than in the connections between people. As a result, the inclination is to attempt changes on individuals rather than systems. Sociological explanations, while not discounting variations in individuals, focus greater levels of attention on the structural and cultural contexts in which behavior takes place.

One example of this individualistic orientation can be illustrated by the tendency to understand criminal behavior in terms of the characteristics of people who commit crimes, rather than the social structures that create crimes. No doubt, motivations such as greed play some role in creating crime, but there are other contributing factors as well, factors that exist independent of the criminal's personality traits. For example, one sociological concern is understanding which types of behaviors are classified as crimes and how these definitions affect social relations. Interestingly, there are a variety of behaviors that have been considered deviant or criminal, such as prostitution (Jenesse 1993), homosexuality (Spector and Kitsuse 1987), or alcohol consumption during Prohibition (Gusfield 1963), even though these behaviors victimize nobody. Once a behavior is identified as a crime, new groups of criminals are created and agents of social control (i.e., police and courts) react to these people accordingly. Once these laws are repealed, as is the case of homosexuality and alcohol consumption in the United States (and, in some locales, prostitution), criminality is extinguished.

Another set of sociological questions concerning criminal behavior that transcend individualistic orientations explores the ways in which individuals are treated once they are identified as having engaged in crime. According to Reiman (1995), poor people are more likely to be apprehended for crimes and, once apprehended, they are more likely to be convicted and be more severely punished than affluent people. Reiman forcefully argues that the types of crimes committed by poor people (i.e., burglary and drug sales) actually cost society less than the crimes committed primarily by the rich. Consider, for instance, the difference in the treatment of burglars and embezzlers. Burglary is the type of crime committed by poor people, and involves sneaking into houses and businesses to steal another person's property. Embezzlement, a crime mainly of the rich, involves sneaking into company financial accounts and stealing corporate finances. Embezzlement is a more lucrative form of crime than burglary, and therefore one would expect more severe penalties for the embezzler. The opposite is the norm. Of those people apprehended for burglary, 82% serve time in prison and are sentenced to an average of 63 months in jail. Of those prosecuted for embezzlement, only 31% serve time in prison and the average sentence is only 16 months in jail (Reiman 1995). These findings imply that once a definition of a crime is created, it does not necessarily mean that all individuals within society will be treated fairly or equitably. Clearly, understanding crime in society requires much more than simply focusing on the individuals who are committing the criminal acts, it also requires examining the judicial processes involved in locating, prosecuting, and punishing criminals. Solving the crime problem necessarily requires more than educating, punishing, or giving therapy to criminals.

Similarly, understanding what goes on in college society requires more than studying the traits of the students, professors, administrators, and support staff that comprise its members. Let's pose a new question concerning college society why some students do well and others do less well. On an individual level, success in college could be explained by the combination of effort and talent. Students who are very smart and who work very hard tend to do well; students who work less hard or who are less talented tend to do more poorly. If college society operates as a **meritocracy,** where people rise and fall in the system according to their individual merits, these factors would offer a comprehensive explanation of variations in success between students. However, sociological studies of education systems reveal that our schools operate in a less than meritocratic fashion (Bowles and Gintis 1976).

One of the most important factors that influence educational success is the degree to which a student's family has access to capital. **Capital** is anything that can be traded for financial value. There are multiple forms of capital, and each contributes to the educational experiences of students. Unlike talent and effort, which are traits of individuals, large proportions of capital are inherited and are intricately linked to the economic relationships of a student's family to the larger society. According to the French sociologist, Pierre Bourdieu (1977), these relationships have a powerful influence on educational success and later socioeconomic attainment. Of particular importance is the degree to which parents can extend economic capital, social capital, and cultural capital to their children.

Economic capital comprises existing monetary assets or tangible possessions. These can be in the form of savings accounts, a home that can be mortgaged or sold, and possession of consumer goods such as books or computers. Obviously the child raised in a family that can afford educational resources will have better opportunities to prepare for a college education. Economic capital is also invested in students at the community level. In 1996, for example, the average elementary or secondary school student in New York state received $8700 in funding from state and local sources. In contrast, students in Mississippi received less than half this level of support, $3,670 (Morgan & Morgan 1997). Not surprisingly, in 1996 the percentage of New Yorkers who had college degrees (26.3%) was considerably higher than that of Mississippi residents (17.6%) (Morgan and Morgan 1997). This is not to say that it is impossible for an able person from a poor background to get into a prestigious college and to do well there. It is important, though, to consider how the economic position of students from disadvantaged backgrounds poses barriers not faced by students from more affluent backgrounds (Berliner and Biddle 1997; Kozol 1991). Economic capital not only influences the degree of preparation students receive for a college education, it also sorts students into different institutions in accordance with their abilities to pay for their education. While members of all social classes are represented in different types of colleges, members of the upper-middle and upper classes are disproportionately concentrated in expensive private universities, members of the middle class locate themselves in less expensive state colleges, and members of the lower class are concentrated in community colleges (Baker and Velez 1996). This works like a large sorting machine, eventually funneling students from privileged backgrounds into lucrative and high-prestige jobs, those from the middle class into moderate-paying positions, and those from the lower class into lower-paying technical jobs. Colleges simply mediate this process.

Social capital comprises networks of relationships that can be mobilized for economic gain (Bourdieu 1977). In most circumstances, people who are connected with the power-holders in society have a decided advantage over those who lack these connections. At some of the most prestigious universities, for instance, legacies (applicants whose parents attended the university) are given preferential consideration in the application process. Social capital, such as this, is especially important to consider when evaluating the effect a college education has on subsequent success, as elite universities connect students to power-holders. As a consequence of entering into prestigious colleges, students are afforded better opportunities to cultivate relationships that can be exchanged for financial success, such as working as a page for a congressman or landing an internship on a nationally syndicated television show. These opportunities, in turn, connect students with other high-powered individuals. Students at these schools are also able to generate friendships with fellow students, people who will likely be the future leaders of business and government. The payoffs for attending the right college can be substantial, and many of these payoffs come from the social relationships developed, not just simply because of the educational programs offered.

Cultural capital consists of the ability to interact in a manner that is customary to the more privileged members in society. According to Bourdieu (1984), there are remarkable differences in the ways in which lower-class, middle-class, and upper-class members of society view and interact with the world. Vocabularies differ by social class, for instance, as do hobbies and tastes. If a person can understand and interact in ways that are familiar to members of the upper class, to "fit in," he or she stands a greater chance of entering these networks and receiving subsequent rewards. Bourdieu (1977) and others (Bowles and Gintis 1976; MacLeod 1987; Willis 1977) found that schools tend to put the interests of the upper classes as focal points in the curriculum. They also found that teachers tend to grade students more favorably if they can express their ideas in the same manner as members of the upper-middle class and upper class (Bernstein 1977). Doing well in school, therefore, is not just a matter of having good ideas or learning the material. It also hinges on learning material that tends to be oriented to the interests of privileged members of society, as well as being able to express ideas in ways that resonate with people who hold this status.

The curriculum of some college programs offers interesting illustrations of cultural capital in action. At Cornell University, for instance, wine tasting is one of the most popular courses on campus, offering a poignant example of what cultural capital theorists point to as a class bias in the curriculum. Wine, it should be remembered, is a beverage highly valued by members of the upper-middle and upper classes. In contrast, one would be hard pressed to locate a college that offers a beer-tasting class, beer being the alcoholic beverage of choice for the working class. Once enrolled in wine tasting, those students who are already familiar with the customs of wine consumption (those coming from more privileged backgrounds) will have an obvious advantage over those who have less familiarity. Of course this is a comparatively trivial example, but it does illustrate a common tendency within many courses to valorize the interests and perspectives of the upper classes. Once the curriculum is structured toward that group, members of the lower classes will have a more difficult time achieving comparable levels of success.

The roles that the various forms of capital have on influencing success in college and society often go unrecognized because of a cultural tendency to reduce complex problems to the characteristics of the individuals that make up society. Clearly, doing well in college is influenced by factors completely outside the meritocracy myth that posits that success is simply the result of personal efforts and talent. Aside from being a limited way of understanding the world, individualistic orientations have an impact on approaches to remedying personal and social crises. Instead of focusing on individuals who make up college and society, the sociological imagination stretches the mind to think in very different ways about personal and social experiences.

Colleges as Total Institutions

The sociological imagination also involves being able to observe the familiar transformed in its meaning (Berger 1963). College society, for many, is familiar terrain. Its contours are so well known that much of it is taken for granted. One advantage of linking college society to other institutions is that it helps us to see it, and the workings of these other institutions, in new ways. Erving Goffman's classic *Asylums* (1961) revealed features of college society that are remarkably similar to mental hospitals. From Goffman's perspective, colleges and other boarding schools can be understood as **total institutions,** self-contained societies that are designed to service all the needs of the people residing within their boundaries. When viewed this way, colleges become comparable to other total institutions, such as old age homes, orphanages, mental hospitals, TB sanatoria, leprosaria, jails, POW camps, Army boot camps, monasteries, and cloisters.

In a total institution, all aspects of life are conducted in the same place under the same single authority. For example, prisons are supervised by wardens, mental hospitals are supervised by chief psychiatrists, and colleges are led by presidents. These authority figures have tremendous power to determine the types of conduct that will be permitted within the institution's confines. They also have the power to mete out punishment to transgressors who break the rules and regulations of the institution. Total institutions are also largely self-contained and are designed so that day-to-day interaction can occur independent of the outside society. The monastery, for instance, serves as a retreat from the outside world, and as a consequence is structured so that the outside contact available to monks is minimal. Similarly, most student needs are met on campus, including health care, food, housing, athletic facilities, and entertainment. As a consequence of building these structures into college society, students are structurally discouraged from interacting with people outside of its confines.

Within total institutions, inmates are serviced in the immediate company of large groups of other inmates and all are treated in a like manner. For example, mental patients and prisoners are fed collectively and bedtimes are strictly enforced. In college society, students are expected to take examinations collectively, attend classes according to schedules, and are processed in assembly-line-like fashion during registration. This scheduling is, to a great extent, a product of the needs of servicing large numbers of people within the institution's confines.

One of the most salient characteristics of total institutions is the strongly imposed division between the inmates (prisoners, mental patients, students) and the staff (guards, psychiatrists, professors). According to Goffman, inmates and staff tend to see each other in terms of narrow and sometimes hostile stereotypes. From the perspective of inmates, the staff is often viewed as condescending, high-handed, and mean. From the perspective of the staff, inmates are generally seen as untrustworthy and irresponsible. As a consequence, the staff tends to feel superior and righteous in their encounters with inmates. Given the power staff have to control inmates' lives, they also tend to structure encounters to reinforce inmates' self-definitions as inferior and blame worthy. It is also interesting to note that all total institutions discourage informal interaction, except in tightly controlled circumstances, between the inmates and the staff. Consider, for instance, the patterns of encounters between professors and students, which tend to be restricted to class time and office hours. Excessive friendliness or overfamiliarity between professors and students is not encouraged, and it is especially noteworthy to consider the degree to which all total institutions prohibit sexual encounters between the inmates and staff.

Although total institutions are manifestly operated and controlled by the staff according to a system of rational rules, there is ample documentation to show that these rules are frequently broken. In the world of the mental hospital, for example, there exists an under life of clandestine activities in which inmates' acts of subterfuge go unrecognized and/or unacknowledged by the staff (Goffman 1959). This includes stealing food, rendezvousing for sexual encounters, and sneaking away from the institution. Many of these acts are accomplished through a tacit agreement between the staff and the inmates not to invade each others' spaces. In college society, one can see this demonstrated by students' respect for professors' office spaces and, perhaps more importantly, the respect professors show for students' privacy. Only in rare circumstances do professors or other college authorities enter dormitories unannounced. It is no wonder that students are able to circulate old examinations, that alcohol and drugs are readily available, and that illegal activities such as gambling occur on a regular basis in the under life of colleges. It is also little wonder that professors are often very ignorant of what really occurs on campus once they leave for home in the evenings (Moffatt 1989).

As Goffman demonstrated, colleges can be linked with the operations of other organizations that at first glance appear to be very different types of places. By observing the unfamiliar in the familiar, Goffman offers a model to follow in the comparison of college society to organizations that share similar patterns of structure and culture.

Levels of Analysis

It is, upon reflection, an ambitious project to understand the great range of society, from the grand to the minute, from the broad to the narrow, and from the general to the specific. This poses a particularly vexing problem in the present book, which involves drawing parallels between society and colleges. I suggest that colleges are, in many ways, a microcosm of the larger social order. As such they can be used to demonstrate social patterns and processes that are commonplace outside the university confines. However, this opens the possibility for confusion, because in the end, colleges are but one institution in a world system that integrates many other institutions in highly complex ways.

The trick for the sociologist is to concentrate analysis and focus on comparable levels of analysis when drawing comparisons between colleges and society. To focus on a **level of analysis** is to limit the range and complexity of the observations to be examined. In some circumstances, sociological interest is in examining the governmental operations in an entire nation. In other instances, social inquiry concentrates on what happens within small groups of people as they encounter one another. Thus, society can be understood in terms of its lesser and greater degrees of removal from individuals, ranging through the micro-, meso-, and macrolevels of analysis.

The study of face-to-face interaction is called **microlevel analysis** because it occurs between the most fundamental elements of society—people. At the microlevel, the concern is identifying the norms of conduct and the other immediate factors that influence persons or small groups to behave in the manner they do. In college society, examples could include studying face-to-face interaction in the dormitories, classrooms, dining halls, and laboratories. **Mesolevel analysis** concerns the study of entire organizations, such as bureaucracies, offices, and institutions. To understand a college at the mesolevel might require, for instance, analyzing budgetary allotments between departments. It might also necessitate examining the formal policies of the college, such as methods of hiring faculty members and dismissing students. These observations could be especially helpful in understanding the history of any particular bureaucracy, from its genesis to its eventual demise. **Macrolevel analysis** is designed to examine the workings of entire societies and requires linking organizations and individual experience with the larger social order. For example, the large baby-boom generation (born from 1946 to 1964) and the GI Bill (which financially enabled veterans to attend school) had profound effects on the number of students enrolled in colleges (Rothstein 1996). Laws and customs requiring segregated classrooms and the subsequent repeal of these practices produced profound changes as well.

Understanding the parallels between college and society requires intellectual dexterity and the ability to jump from one level of analysis to another, depending on the concerns that are being addressed. I suggest that the same types of microlevel experiences, such as discrimination, that occur in college society also occur in similar patterns in the wider society. Looking at colleges in operation also provides a means of understanding the bureaucratic processes that occur in other complex organizations, such as at IBM or in the military. Perhaps my boldest contention, though, is that life in college society can oftentimes be revealed as operating much like a microcosm of the larger social order, and that society in its great complexity is often illustrated in the workings of rather small institutions.

Looking Ahead: Framing College Society through Sociological Perspectives

Each of the chapters that follow are designed to be complete in and of themselves, and can be thought of as empirically grounded essays on college and society. They are not studies in the sense of being independent research projects of the form that are commonly published in research journals, which are primarily intended for a professional audience. Instead, I try to offer accessible appraisals of college life as seen from particular vantage points or perspectives. I also offer definitions of important concepts, so that newcomers to the discipline of sociology can not only learn the perspectives, but also the terminology sociologists use to converse with one another about social behavior.

One challenge in introducing sociology and the sociological imagination is that the discipline lacks a uniform agreement on how best to understand the workings of society. In reality, there is no singular sociology or sociological perspective, but rather a multitude of sociological perspectives. **Perspectives** can be understood as points of view or lenses that guide our perceptions of reality (Charon 1995). Perspectives develop because they help people generate a useful system to give the world a sense of order.

In any randomly selected group of sociologists, there are likely to be people who frame their understandings of the world in very different ways. To offer some means of appreciating the diversity of perspectives, and the varieties of insights they offer, each chapter in this book adopts a different perspective while examining a different facet of college society. To foreshadow, as well as to provide an initial understanding of some of the different visions held by sociologists, the following offers a brief overview of some of these perspectives and their application in this book.

The Symbolic Interactionist Perspective

Symbolic interactionism, a theory largely attributed to the teachings of George Herbert Mead (1934), examines the dynamics of face-to-face encounters in order to explain social interaction. Central to this perspective is the appreciation of the cognitive processes involved in creating successful interaction, particularly the ability of people to create and manipulate symbols. Toward this end, symbolic interactionists tend to concentrate on the meanings different situations have for people and how their responses correspond with their definitions of reality.

Symbolic interactionists, particularly those studying dramaturgy (Goffman 1959), see considerable merit in the metaphor once posed by William Shakespeare: "All the world's a stage, And all the men and women merely players..." According to symbolic interactionists, people are placed in "roles" and "perform" social acts. As actors, people think ahead in order to form impressions on others and use language, props, and teams to define their reality. Once these definitions are created and accepted, encounters become predictable and meaningful for the participants.

Chapter 2 uses the symbolic interactionist perspective to understand the events surrounding fraternity hazing. By looking at the social relationships in fraternities, and the rites of passage imposed through the pledging process, this perspective underscores the reasons why people sometimes do very irrational things. In this case, what compels fraternity members to perpetrate abuse and why do pledges submit to abusive acts? Symbolic interactionism reveals a variety of social forces that shape these encounters, as well as possibilities to ameliorate the problem of hazing on college campuses.

The Feminist Perspective

Feminist scholars focus on the ways in which social systems commonly fail to serve the needs of women and the ways in which women's contributions to society are undervalued (Rhode 1997). By concentrating on gender, feminists call attention to the ways in which social experiences and gender roles are intricately related: for instance, the ways in which child-rearing responsibilities are allocated have influenced women's economic attainment. Feminists also focus on the degree to which men and women are socialized to have different values, as well as the ways in which women are systematically discriminated against in society.

Chapter 3 examines the issue of gender inequality on college campuses. Although society is commonly portrayed as being based on equality of opportunity, plentiful evidence suggests that women face a number of cultural and structural barriers to attaining economic equality with men, and these barriers are revealed on college campuses. College society contributes to a process that began long before students arrived on campus, a process that funnels boys and girls into gendered roles. It also illustrates the experiences of men and women once they enter the workforce, situations that result in women's lower earnings and slower advancement up career ladders. The difficulties of responding to social inequities are illustrated by the ways in which college campuses are reacting to the gender problem.

The Organizational Perspective

The organizational perspective, introduced by Max Weber (Gerth and Mills 1946), concentrates on the operations of bureaucracies and the means by which these organizations achieve technical efficiency. The organizational perspective is also commonly tied to critical analyses of how these bureaucratic processes influence the culture of society and the relationships between members of society.

College society is analyzed as a complex bureaucracy in Chapter 4. Under this lens, college society is framed to reveal strong similarities to the ways businesses and governmental organizations operate. These similarities reflect enduring observations about bureaucracies—that as they create technologically efficient ways of processing people, they also create cultures that systematically dehumanize people. The question for consideration is how to expand and retain the efficiency these complex organizations provide, as well as shape them to enable the liberation, rather than debasement, of the human experience.

Conflict and Functionalist Perspectives

Conflict theorists believe that society is best characterized as a place of conflict or war. As Marx said in the *Manifesto of the Communist Party* (1848/1972) "the history of all hitherto existing societies is a history of class struggle." From the conflict perspective, understanding society requires identifying the different coalitions and their competing efforts to control resources. Often, these competitions result in the losing side becoming disenfranchised, exploited, and abused. The victors, on the other hand, accumulate wealth, status, and power, and develop rationalizations of why they deserve more than the losing side.

Conflict theorists tend to offer critical appraisals of the impact of social inequality. Rather than seeing inequality as inevitable or desirable, they tend to focus on ways inequality undermines the well-being of groups who have little power or wealth. They also focus attention on the ways in which inequality undermines the potential of all groups to produce humane, trusting, and cooperative relationships with one another. Stemming from its roots in Marxian sociology, conflict theory also strives to create a society in which the degree of inequality is leveled, often by linking their research activities and teaching with political activism (see Freire 1994).

In contrast to conflict theorists, functionalists tend to focus their attention to a greater extent on social harmony than on social conflict. This theoretical approach was introduced to sociology through the writings of Emile Durkheim (1895/1964), particularly in his seminal book *Division of Labor in Society*. Durkheim suggested that society is much like a living body, with each component part charged with a specific task. Just as the brain is in charge of thinking, schools are charged with educating citizens. Just as the stomach is charged with digestion, economies are charged with distributing resources. Other institutions necessary for society include the family (nurtures children), religion (instills values), and government (enforces social order).

From a functionalist perspective, all of the institutions in society are linked in systems that tend toward homeostasis or balance. If one institution changes, other institutions will be affected and adjust themselves to keep the entire system in balance. Should systems not be able to adjust, society experiences pathology. Living bodies show pathology through fevers, stomachaches, and death. Societies show pathology through things such as increased suicide rates, crime rates, and unemployment.

This perspective also highlights the mechanisms by which society fits people into its existing systems and services their needs. Durkheim once explained his appreciation for this capability of society, noting with wonder that each morning he could awaken and expect to have a fresh bottle of milk on his doorstep. Functionalists such as Durkheim view these simple events as great accomplishments stemming from complex systems that link people and organizations with one another.

Chapter 5 uses sports in college society to highlight the contrasting visions that the conflict and functionalist theorists have in understanding social relations. Both perspectives reveal that sports are anything but a trivial part of college society, or society as a whole. Functionalists suggest that sports serve a vital function in integrating the society as a whole. In contrast, conflict theorists argue that sports serve to legitimate inequality in society.

By comparing these two perspectives, the positive and counterproductive aspects of sports are highlighted, offering direction for the construction of policies for college athletics.

The Merits of Shifting Perspectives

Like a gestalt experiment that presents a picture that at one moment looks like a vase and the next moment like two people facing one another, adopting different perspectives shapes and reshapes interpretations of observations. This is not to say that all perspectives are of equal value in all circumstances. The trick for sociologists is to adopt a perspective that offers a useful means of encapsulating and describing the workings of society. In some circumstances, symbolic interactionism offers a more parsimonious approach for understanding social relationships than conflict theory. In other circumstances, the reverse will be true. Also, perspectives can be merged with one another. For instance, a study of women in poverty could be well served by both a feminist and a conflict theory approach.

The variety of perspectives opens great possibilities for sociologists to create appreciation for the complexity of society, as well as create a sense of order from this complexity. Rather than accepting one perspective and doggedly forcing observations of college society within that framework, I have chosen instead to highlight the ways in which college society can be understood through different perspectives. Having armed readers with this repertoire of perspectives, this book concludes with a chapter outlining different methodologies that they can use to contribute to the study of college and society. The hope is to stir the sociological imagination and stimulate budding sociologists to examine familiar surroundings in new ways, as well as equip them with the skills to examine the workings of society.

REFERENCES

Baker, Theresa and William Velez. 1996. "Access to and Opportunity in Postsecondary Education in the United States: A Review." *Sociology of Education.* 69:82–101.

Bellah, Robert, Richard Madsen, William Sullivan, Ann Swidler, and Steven Tipton. 1985. *Habits of the Heart: Individualism and Commitment in American Life.* New York: Harper and Row.

Berger, Peter. 1963. *Invitation to Sociology: A Humanistic Perspective.* Garden City, New York: Anchor Books.

Berliner, David and Bruce Biddle. 1997. *The Manufactured Crisis.* White Plains, New York: Longman.

Bernstein, Basil. 1977. "Social Class, Language, and Socialization." Pp 487–510 in *Power and Ideology in Education,* edited by Jerome Karabel and A. H. Halsey. New York: Oxford University Press.

Bourdieu, Pierre. 1977. "Cultural Reproduction and Social Reproduction." Pp 487–510 in *Power and Ideology in Education*, edited by Jerome Karabel and A. H. Halsey. New York: Oxford University Press.

Bourdieu, Pierre. 1984. *Distinction: A Social Critique of the Judgement of Taste*. Cambridge, MA: Harvard University Press.

Bowles, Samuel and Herbert Gintis. 1976. *Schooling in Capitalist America*. New York: Basic Books.

Charon, Joel. 1995. *Symbolic Interactionism: An Introduction, Interpretation and Integration*. 5th Edition. Englewood Cliffs, NJ: Prentice Hall.

Coontz, Stephanie. 1992. *The Way We Never Were: American Families and the Nostalgia Trap*. New York: Basic Books.

Durkheim, Emile. 1951 [1897]. *Suicide*. New York: The Free Press.

Durkheim, Emile. 1964 [1895]. *The Division of Labor in Society*. New York: Free Press.

Elder, Glen. 1999. *Children of the Great Depression*.

Freire, Paulo. 1994. *Pedagogy of the Oppressed*. New York: Continuum.

Gergen, Kenneth. 1991. *The Saturated Self: Dilemmas of Identity in Contemporary Life*. New York: Basic Books.

Gerth, H. H. and C. Wright Mills (eds). 1946. *From Max Weber: Essays in Sociology*. New York: Oxford University Press.

Goffman, Erving. 1959. *The Presentation of Self in Everyday Life*. Garden City, NY: Anchor Books.

Goffman, Erving. 1961. *Asylums*. Garden City, NY: Anchor Books.

Gusfield, Joseph. 1963. *Symbolic Crusade: Status Politics and the Urban Temperance Movement*. Chicago: University of Illinois.

Homans, George. 1974. *Social Behavior. Its Elementary Forms (2nd Edition)*. New York: Harcourt Brace Jovanovich.

Jenesse, Valerie. 1963. *Making It Work: The Prostitutes' Rights Movement in Perspective*. New York: Aldine de Gruyter.

Kozol, Jonathan. 1991. *Savage Inequalities: Children in America's Schools*. New York: Harper Perennial.

Marchant, Gregory and Isadore Newman. 1994. "Faculty Activities and Rewards: Views from Education Administrators in the USA." *Assessment and Evaluation in Higher Education*. 19:14–152.

Marshall, Ray and Marc Tucker. 1992. *Thinking for a Living: Education and the Wealth of Nations*. New York: Basic Books.

Marx, Karl and Friedrich Engels. 1972 [1848]. "Manifesto of the Communist Party." in Tucker, Robert C., [ed.], *The Marx-Engels Reader*. New York: Norton.

McLeod, Jay. 1987. *Ain't No Makin' It*. Boulder: Westview Press.

Mead, George Herbert. 1934. *Mind, Self and Society*. Chicago: University of Chicago Press.

Mills, C. Wright. 1959. *The Sociological Imagination*. New York: Oxford University Press.

Moffatt, Michael. 1989. *Coming of Age in New Jersey: College and American Culture*. New, Brunswick, NJ: Rutgers University Press.

Morgan, Kathleen and Scott Morgan. 1997. *State Rankings 1997*. Lawrence, KS: Morgan Quitno.

Reiman, Jeffrey. 1995. *The Rich Get Richer and the Poor Get Prison: Ideology, Class and Criminal Justice*. Boston: Allyn & Bacon.

Rhode, Deborah. 1997. *Speaking of Sex: The Denial of Gender Inequality*. Cambridge, MA: Harvard University Press.

Ritzer, George. 1996. *The McDonaldization of Society*. Thousand Oaks, CA: Pine Forge Press.

Rosovsky, Henry. 1990. *The University: An Owner's Manual*. New York: W. W. Norton.

Rothstein, Stanley. 1996. *Schools and Society*. Englewood Cliffs: Prentice Hall.

Schor, Juliet. 1998. *The Overspent American: Upscaling, Downshifting, and the New Consumer.* New York: Basic Books.

Spector, Malcolm and John Kitsuse. 1987. *Constructing Social Problems.* New York: Aldine De Gruyter.

Thompson, E. P. 1967. "Time, Work-Discipline, and Industrial Capitalism." *Past and Present.* 38:56–97.

Tocqueville, Alexis de. 1969 [1836]. *Democracy in America.* New York: Doubleday.

U.S. Census Bureau. 1999. *Statistical Abstract of the United States: 1999.* Washington, DC.

Willis, Paul. 1977. *Learning to Labor.* Aldershot: Gower.

2

Fraternity Hazing

Insights from the Symbolic Interactionist Perspective

Less than a mile from my former office sits the Theta Chi fraternity house. On February 10, 1997, seventeen-year-old Clarkson University freshman Binaya "Bini" Oja, along with twenty other students, began pledging Theta Chi fraternity. As part of their initiation, the pledges gathered in a semicircle around a bucket and were instructed by fraternity members to take turns drinking hard liquor. If the pledges did not drink the liquor fast enough so that bubbles were seen rising in the bottles, they were also instructed to guzzle a full glass of beer. The point of the game was simple—each pledge was expected to drink until he vomited.

Bini drank a lot and was carried upstairs. The next morning he was discovered dead with his feet up on a couch and his face on the floor next to a garbage can. An autopsy determined that he died as a consequence of inhaling his own vomit. Six months later, on the same day that the Clarkson University task force on fraternities announced its programs to counter hazing, a similar incident happened at Louisiana State University. Benjamin Wynne, a pledge at Sigma Alpha Epsilon fraternity, died during a fraternity initiation ritual. His autopsy revealed a blood alcohol content of .588, a level six times that of the legal limit.

If Bini's and Benjamin's deaths had been isolated incidents, they probably would not warrant much sociological examination. Accidents happen and people occasionally engage in foolish acts. The book *Broken Pledges: The Deadly Rite of Hazing* (Nuwer 1990), however, clearly documents that pledging abuses are common in fraternities, sororities, and military academies. To give some idea of the variety of abuses occurring as students pledge fraternities and sororities, here are just three examples, quoted from *Broken Pledges*:

1974: Monmouth College, West Long Branch, New Jersey; Zeta Beta Tau
Members ordered five pledges to dig six-foot "graves" on a sandy beach on the Atlantic Ocean. The five then lay down in the graves while members threw handfuls of sand atop them. The grave of William E. Flowers, Jr. collapsed, and he began inhaling sand. He died of asphyxiation. A grand jury called the death

"accidental," clearing seven Zeta Beta Tau members who had been arrested on charges of manslaughter. (1990; 299)

1980: Stetson University, Deland, Florida; Pi Kappa Psi
Several members of the Chi Chapter were expelled from the fraternity for shocking pledges with an electrical device. Seven years later the entire chapter was suspended for one year in a similar incident, possibly involving the same electrical device. (1990; 303)

1986: Manhattan College, Bronx, New York; Beta Sigma
On one of the coldest nights of the winter, pledge Michael Flynn, nineteen, was abandoned naked on an isolated country road in Putnam County, New York. During the drive by automobile to the drop-off point, fraternity brothers poured beer on his feet, ignoring two pleas from Flynn that his feet were freezing. The wind-chill factor outside the car was thirty-five degrees below zero. Flynn's feet were seriously frostbitten. He was hospitalized for two weeks and suffered permanent health problems. A judge acquitted the four defendants, saying he could not determine the brothers had knowingly subjected Flynn to frostbite. (1990; 313).

Especially common in fraternity hazing are situations in which pledges are pressured to drink shots of alcohol in rapid succession. In other circumstances pledges are blindfolded and dropped off in remote areas, sometimes during the middle of winter, sometimes naked. Pledges have been compelled to perform raids on sorority houses, stealing kisses, groping, and ripping clothes. Some fraternities require pledges to perform rigorous calisthenics, sometimes in heavy clothing (Nuwer 1990; Sanday 1990). In the context of discussions with current and former members of Greek organizations, I learned of toes being broken by hammers in games of fear, beatings with paddles, sleep deprivation, submersions in vats of filth, and drinking "games."

It is difficult to provide an accurate assessment of the frequency of hazing. One literature review found over 400 documented hazing incidents resulting in serious injury and death from 1900 to 1990 (Nuwer 1990). Certainly this underestimates how often it occurs. A survey of 283 fraternity advisors revealed that over half of these advisors believed that hazing existed in some of their groups (Shaw and Morgan 1990). Hazing is not limited to college campuses, of course. A report to the Senate Committee on Armed Services found that hazing of "plebes," the incoming recruits to military academies, was also very common (U.S. Government Accounting Office 1992). There are a variety of reasons why hazing is underreported. Fraternities are secretive organizations and pledges are required to keep oaths of silence concerning initiation procedures (Leemon 1972). Students often do not recognize when they are being hazed or abused (Moffatt 1989). Colleges and universities sometimes avoid publicizing hazing incidents for fear of damaging institutional reputations or incurring financial liability to victims (Curry 1989; Nuwer 1990).

The concern of this chapter is not to indict fraternities. In fact, these organizations can be characterized by many positive features, not least of which are community service work and the sense of belonging they provide for their members. The concern is to understand why individuals such as Bini Oja, Benjamin Wynne, Chuck Stenzel, Michael Flynn, and William Flowers would willingly participate in the events leading up to their own injury and death. It is also to understand why hazing is integrated into fraternity subculture and why brothers inflict psychological and physical pain on their recruits.

On the surface, these acts appear at worst, sadistic, and at best, stupid. These terms, however, are flawed because they attribute the source of these problems as being within individuals rather than stemming from the interactional processes that happen between people. Sadism, for example, implies the existence of a psychological or moral abnormality in the character of the fraternity brothers or pledges. Although published accounts indicate that some hazed pledges had difficulty adjusting to college life, most appear to be normal, healthy young men (Nuwer 1990). Sadism also suggests that fraternity brothers harbor hostility toward the pledges. In fact, the opposite is true. Fraternity brothers tend to care very deeply for their pledges and feel great regret when a pledge is seriously injured, as was the case with the members of Theta Chi.

The term *stupidity* implies that fraternity members and pledges are of below average intelligence. Data do not seem to support the contention that hazing is a product of low intelligence or ignorance. As evidence of this, I compared the grade point averages of fraternity members and non-fraternity members while I served on the Greek Life Task Force at the State University of New York at Potsdam. I found no difference between the grade point averages of Greeks (pledges and members) and their non-Greek counterparts. This task force also found that Greek members have a high level of awareness of what constitutes hazing, as well as the legal consequences of infractions of hazing policy. With these insights in mind, it is apparent that the source of hazing problems is not the result of personality or intellectual shortcomings of pledges or fraternity members.

These observations suggest that fraternity hazing is not so much a problem of individuals as it is a problem of social relationships. To gain further understanding of the power social relationships have on shaping personal behavior, this chapter reframes observations surrounding fraternity hazing within the symbolic interactionist perspective. From this perspective, rather than focusing on the personality quirks of the victims or perpetrators of hazing, a higher priority is placed on the social context in which hazing events take place.

Pledging as a Rite of Passage

The typical college student only resides in the college community for a few short years, before moving on to other endeavors. This presents fraternities and sororities with an ongoing problem of keeping their organizations thriving and intact in an environment where almost all potential members are transitory. Within a very limited time span, fraternities and sororities need to be able to select groups of nonmembers (independents) and recruit them to full membership status (Greeks). Once independents are recruited and initiated to full membership status, the continued survival of fraternities and sororities rests on their members' abilities and motivations to replenish themselves with the initiation of a new group of recruits.

Fraternities and sororities are not the only types of organization or institution to face this type of concern. For example, the institution of marriage rests on the creation of a sense of strong loyalty between spouses. In western society, this loyalty does not emerge overnight, but builds through courtship rituals. Training programs for some professions, such as physicians, are structured to create a strong sense of commitment to the group as well. The same holds true for the military, which, in very short order, creates loyal soldiers out of mere citizens. Anthropological studies reveal that all of these groups, fraternities and sororities included, adopt initiation rites that are sociologically similar to the rites of passage of traditional tribal groups (Leemon 1972).

Initiation rites, according to the classic study by Arnold van Gennep (1909) *Les Rites de Passage,* occur in three phases: (1) separation, (2) transition, (3) incorporation. The first step in an initiation rite involves a selection of candidates to undergo the rites and garnering their commitment to a process that has yet to ensue. According to van Gennep, this occurs during the **separation phase,** a brief period when a large pool of potential candidates becomes reduced to a select few. Not every college student is a suitable candidate for fraternity life, just as not every available man is a suitable marriage partner for every available woman. The separation phase requires accomplishing two complementary concerns. First, the fraternity presents itself as attractive, so that the desired candidates become interested in joining the organization. Second, the fraternity screens out undesirable candidates.

This selection process is performed during "rushing," a period when prospective pledges are asked to visit the fraternity houses. During rushing, fraternity and sorority members extol the virtues of fraternity or sorority membership, informing candidates that membership offers instant belonging in a social network of "brothers" and "sisters" who "look out for one another." For college students lacking strong social networks, this can make Greek life particularly appealing, especially if it also offers assistance in generating romantic encounters or access to parties. Prospective members are also shown the advantages of off-campus housing and the increased freedom it can offer. For the right type of student, fraternities are very attractive organizations.

Rushing also enables Greek organizations to screen out people who have lower prospects of becoming committed members. One way fraternities and sororities do this is by selecting candidates that fit consistent standards based on race, class, gender, and physical attractiveness (Strombler 1994). This first phase in fraternity initiation rites has very strong parallels with the earliest phases of courtship, the period when dating partners screen one other during casual encounters, keeping their options open for a suitable match for a long-term relationship. While engaged in this screening, both parties try to make themselves appear as appealing as possible, thereby increasing their chances for attracting the most suitable match.

At the end of rushing, independents are formally asked if they will pledge the fraternity. If candidates agree to pledge, they enter into the transition phase of the initiation rites. The **transition phase** marks a status shift, when the candidates can no longer consider themselves independent of the group, but nor can they consider themselves members either. This quasi-membership status in fraternities is comparable to the status of fiancé in a courtship relationship. After the acceptance of a marriage proposal, for instance, an engagement ring is worn to signify one's change in status. Upon the acceptance of a bid, pledges are given pledge pins and other symbols of the organization, and are asked to swear oaths of loyalty and secrecy. In both cases, pledges and fiancés are aligned and joined with their partners, but still lack the rights and responsibilities that are accorded their fully initiated counterparts.

Entry into the transition phase is a positive one, but it also marks the onset of a period of ongoing tests, whereby the potential members are evaluated as to whether they will serve as faithful and capable members. Fraternities commonly assign a pledge master or "whip" to supervise the pledge class and to create a sense of loyalty to their fellow pledges and the fraternity (Leemon 1972). One way that the whip generates this group loyalty is by assigning tasks, which can range from comparatively trivial assignments (i.e., learning the Greek alphabet) to more difficult activities. Paradoxically, as the fraternity places more severe expectations upon pledges, pledges tend to respond by perceiving the fraternity membership as ever more exclusive and desirable.

Hazing tends to occur during the transition phase, when pledges' loyalties are being tested. For example, Sanday (1990) documents one fraternity that required its pledges to strip from the waist down and to tie a thick string around their genitals. They were then told to tie the other end of the string around a rock. Pledges were then blindfolded and instructed to throw the rock with all their might. Unbeknownst to them, however, the fraternity members cut the strings after the pledges were blindfolded. On the surface, this act appears simply cruel, but in the context of initiation rites, it becomes apparent that it is designed to evaluate the pledges' willingness to submit to group expectations.

Finally, according to van Gennep's model, pledges are incorporated into the fraternity in a final swearing in. The **incorporation phase** is akin to the wedding ceremony, where the individuals' status officially changes to full membership in the group. Few people outside of Greek organizations actually know how these final initiation rites take place. In fact, in one of the most detailed analyses of fraternity initiation rites (Leemon 1972), the investigator was allowed to witness all aspects of the pledging procedure except this final ceremony. He could only report that the initiates returned from the room looking simultaneously drained and elated.

Initiation rites are important to consider when analyzing fraternity hazing, because they are responsible for changing pledges' identities and loyalties. At each phase of the initiation rite, pledges are sent messages to think of themselves not in relation to their college, their parents, or their friends, but rather in relation to the fraternity. This does not occur by accident; it happens by design. The pledges' prospects for becoming persons with new values and loyalties are altered once the initiation rites begin during the separation phase. During the transition phase they are reshaped, molded, and sculpted into fraternity men. Finally, at the incorporation phase they are initiated as full members. By the end of the initiation, students have been molded into fraternity members, adopt the values and codes of conduct expected of these members, and are capable of recruiting and shaping new members in the next year's pledge class. Building on these insights, the symbolic interactionist perspective reveals how these rites transform the ways in which individuals understand their relationships with others and their selves.

Symbolic Interactionist Theory

Probably more than any other individual, Herbert Blumer (1969) is responsible for introducing the symbolic interactionist perspective to mainstream sociology in a series of articles, later published in his book *Symbolic Interactionism: Perspective and Method.* Although not the first symbolic interactionist, Blumer was the first sociologist to use the term *symbolic interactionism* as a way of linking a number of sociological studies into a theoretical whole. The research interests of symbolic interactionists vary, and their studies address a wide range of issues, but there are a set of common premises that link symbolic interactionists with one another. These premises include:

1. Human beings act toward things on the basis of the meanings these things have for them.
2. The meanings of things arise out of the social interaction people have with each other.
3. People engage in interpretation when dealing with the things they encounter (Blumer 1969).

Symbolic interactionists challenge many of the taken-for-granted under-standings of human behavior, particularly the notion that people are made up of enduring personality traits. It is commonly believed that society is made up of particular types of persons, and that these people are consistent in their values and responses from one situation to the next. In contrast, sym-bolic interactionists assert that the self is highly malleable and can be shaped and reshaped. The self is anything but stable, and it has great potential to become something new and different. In fact, to be more accurate, according to the symbolic interactionist perspective, the self is better characterized as a process than an object. It is something that is constructed through an ongo-ing process of interpretation and interaction.

Shifting the imagination in accordance with the symbolic interactionist perspective can be challenging. However, once the perspective is adopted, it opens new horizons and ways of explaining behavior not otherwise sensible. Concepts central to symbolic interactionism can be a useful means of under-standing fraternity hazing. They also provide a means to rethink strategies of curtailing abuses within fraternity initiation rites.

Definitions of Situations

Symbolic interactionists believe that people act towards things in accordance with the meanings things have for them. This insight was introduced to social psychologists by W. I. Thomas (1928), who offered a maxim now com-monly referred to as the **Thomas theorem:** *if people define situations as real, they are real in their consequences.* The Thomas theorem is important not only to understand fraternity hazing but also to understand a wide range of social behavior. The Thomas theorem imposes two questions of concern. First, how is a definition of a situation created? Second, how is a person's behavior in-fluenced by that definition?

Sometimes the definitions exist because of longstanding traditions. For example, in western society, many believe that there will be one true love in their lives, and as a consequence seek a long-term monogamous relationship with a person identified as being their fated match. In other circumstances, definitions of situations are intentionally created by individuals or organiza-tions seeking to advance their interests. This is what politicians call "spin." One way in which spin is accomplished is through the strategic use of lan-guage to redefine situations (Lakoff and Johnson 1980). For example, tobacco companies define cigarette smoking as a "habit" and a "lifestyle," and de-scribe their products as having "flavor." In contrast, critics of cigarette com-panies use terms such as "addiction" and "cancer sticks." Once the words are shifted, the perception of the same object shifts as well.

Fraternities do not tell their pledges that they are going to be "hazed," "beaten," or "abused," but pledges anticipate some degree of abuse during "hell week." Initiation rites are framed as a "tradition" involving "discipline" that is "character-building" and reveals "loyalty" and "commitment." The belief that hazing is part of a tradition is one of the most serious barriers getting fraternity members to reform their initiation procedures. Colleges are also reluctant to frame hazing as a serious problem on their campuses. For example, following the hazing death of Chuck Stenzel, the words *manslaughter* and *abuse* were notably absent from the public addresses of Alfred University officials. These officials were more inclined to use terms such as "accident" or "unfortunate incident." According to Nuwer (1990), so long as hazing remains socially defined as "pranks" or in other benign terms, it will likely continue.

Definitions of situations may also account for some cases of individual and gang rapes that have occurred in fraternity houses. Terms such as "slut" dehumanize the female in the mind of the male, enabling him to avoid thinking of her subjective experiences. Members also avoid feeling guilty by placing blame on the rape victim for the attack, wondering about the type of woman who would allow herself to be so drunk or stoned that she could not say what she wanted. Definitions of situations such as this carry tremendous weight in shaping behaviors of fraternity members and the social responses to their actions (see Martin and Hummer 1989; Nurius, Dimeff & Graham 1996; Rhoads 1995; Sanday 1990; Strombler 1994).

Words are one way to define a situation. Another way to define a situation is to engage in packaging. Packaging involves the systematic linking of symbols and objects together in such a way that perceptions are shaped and managed (Katz 1993). Cigarette companies package their products by linking cigarettes with images of freedom and sexuality, such as the smoker shown on horseback or with a lover cavorting on a blanket. Nazi propaganda films packaged images of Jews with images of rats crawling out of sewers, supporting a cultural definition of Jews as dangerous elements in German society that needed eradication.

How do fraternities package hazing in the context of initiation rites? If fraternity members seek to define a situation as one of solemn importance, rooms are darkened, candles are lit, robes are worn, and fraternity symbols are displayed (Nuwer 1990). Any event that accompanies these cultural symbols, such as having initiates lay down in a coffin, will likely be defined as solemn simply by being coupled with those symbols. Situations can also be defined as festive by using bright lights and music. Once a situation is defined as a party, or in Bini Oja's case "a game," initiates can enjoy the act of drinking to the point of vomiting.

Material Selves and Social Selves

Symbolic interactionists point to the malleable nature of the self, but what exactly is the self? Psychologists tend to locate the self as something that exists within people, and as being comprised of stable traits. In contrast, social psychologists (symbolic interactionists included) see the self as something that is constructed between people. In the first book on social psychology, William James (1890/1983) suggested a radical way of rethinking the self, arguing that a person's self is as much made up of social and material components as it is of inner drives and traits. James' thesis hinged on an acceptance of the fact that the self is not something that exists independent of the social world, rather it is a product of the types of things and people that surround it. From this perspective, if the objects and social relationships that surround the self are changed, the self is likely to change as well.

One component of the self, James suggested, is the material self. The **material self** is constituted by tangible objects that represent who we are as individuals. These objects include things such as the type of car a person drives, clothes, hairstyle, and bank account. These things demonstrate to others, among other things, our political beliefs, our tastes, and our dispositions. As a way of marking who we are, these objects constitute our "identity kits" (Goffman 1959). On the surface, these things seem superficial and unimportant in signifying "who we really are." But on reflection, consider the amount of time and money people spend on grooming, fashions, and other consumer goods. All these things are used to make a statement of who we are. From James' perspective, these material objects also have a power in and of themselves to reshape who we think we are.

A classic study by Phillip Zimbaro (1972), the Stanford prison experiment, documented the overwhelming power that material circumstances have on reshaping a sense of self. This study involved randomly assigning students to be "prisoners" and "guards" in a fictive prison setting. Prisoners were assigned numbers, dressed in smocks, made to wear hair nets, and had chains placed on their ankles. Guards were given uniforms, sunglasses, and whistles. All were placed in a fabricated prison in the basement of a building at Stanford University. Although the students assigned to be prisoners and guards were psychologically comparable with one another at the beginning of the experiment, within three days they had each developed very different personality traits consistent with their prisoner or guard roles. Guards became vindictive and were comfortable in demeaning prisoners in a variety of ways, such as sending them to isolation rooms and spraying them with fire extinguishers. The prisoners complied with the guards' demands, referred to themselves by number rather than by name, and felt little loyalty to one another. The psychological stress was so strong that some prisoners broke down and cried during the course of the experiment, forgetting that it was a fictional prison and that they were not really prisoners. Following the conclusion of the study, the students were interviewed and reported that they had changed their sense of self from that of student to that of prisoner or guard.

The Stanford prison experiment demonstrates that a simple manipulation of the material artifacts available to a person can result in dramatic transformations in that person's self. With this in mind, one can observe how Greek organizations increase their power to reshape pledges' identities through the manipulation of pledges' material selves. During pledging, pledges receive (and are often required to wear) items to mark the fraternity on their identities, such as pledge pins, T-shirts, sweatshirts, rings, books, and paddles bearing the fraternity's insignia. A study of sororities revealed that pledges often build their entire wardrobe around the colors and insignias of their organization (Arthur 1997). This study indicated that the clothing was an essential means by which the initiates and new members bolstered their identity to others in the sorority. When pledges surround themselves with these items, it also enhances the degree to which they embrace the fraternity or sorority as a part of their identity.

James points out that a great deal of any individual's identity is also comprised of his or her social relationships. This **social self,** according to James (1890/1983), comprises the set of relations we have with other people, including our friends, relatives, and business associates. It is worth noting that a sense of self can become inflated if one belongs to a successful group. For example, being a professor at Harvard, a computer engineer at NASA, or a member of a star basketball team can increase an individual's pride simply through association with a prestigious organization (Adler and Adler 1989). Conversely, if an individual is socially affiliated with stigmatized groups, such as welfare recipients or the mentally ill, they often come to feel mortified and contaminated (Goffman, 1961; Snow and Anderson 1993) .

Fraternities expand their power to influence the construction of pledges' new sense of self by deliberately and systematically limiting the pledges' social relationships. Fraternity initiation rites are designed to terminate or curtail many of the associations that pledges previously held outside of that organization. The rigor of pledging leaves little time or energy for maintaining outside social relations, and as a consequence pledges' ties outside of the fraternity are considerably weakened. The pledging process also compels pledges to replace their old friends with their brothers in the fraternity. Fraternities, therefore, fit into a category of greedy organizations (Coser 1974). **Greedy organizations** are groups that set up strong boundaries between members and nonmembers, as well as place strong demands on members' time and loyalty.

With friendships and other relationships severed, and greater amounts of the self invested in the fraternity, the prospect of quitting pledging can be daunting. Even though pledges are free to leave the pledging process at any time, greedy organizations tend to increase "exit costs." One exit cost for withdrawing from the initiation rites is the loss of friendships generated during the pledging process. This concern is exacerbated by the coinciding fact that pledges' other friendships have likely weakened considerably as a consequence of the pledging process. Thus, pledging can produce an inertia and a willingness to tolerate abusive situations that would be untenable if the pledge perceived greater access to alternate social networks.

The Looking-Glass Process

Charles Horton Cooley (1922/1970) expanded upon James' theory of social psychology with the addition of the concept of the **looking-glass self,** a metaphor suggesting that we see ourselves reflected in the responses others make toward us. At its most simple level, the theory suggests that if people consistently yawn or fail to make eye contact when a person talks, that person is likely to come to believe that he or she is uninteresting. Conversely, a person who is given trophies, awards, and praise will be more apt to believe that the self he or she possesses has talent and is worthy. In fact, people often do not know what others think of them; the best they can do is interpret the gestures of others. A yawn, after all, may simply indicate that the other person is tired. The looking-glass, therefore, may be better conceptualized as a clouded mirror. We never know exactly what is going on in another person's mind; the best we can do is make informed judgments about ourselves based on the gestures that we perceive others to be making.

Cooley's (1922/1970) theory suggests that individuals' selves can be built up or brought down, respectively, if others send them signals that they are worthy or unworthy of respect. In an analysis of fraternity initiation rites, Leemon (1972) shows that fraternities intentionally manipulate pledges' definitions of self during initiation. In the early phases of the initiation rites, during rushing and immediately following the acceptance of the pledge bid, fraternity members offer self-affirming gestures to the pledge. They are treated as special people and their egos inflate as a consequence. This also creates a strong attachment to the group. However, once pledges are effectively separated from their old connections outside of the fraternity, members then send pledges clear signals that they are of lesser status than fraternity members. Not only does positive contact decrease, but pledges are systematically degraded: for example, by being called upon to perform cleaning tasks around the house or carry matches for members just in case they need a light.

The looking glass metaphor can offer further insight into why pledges submit to hazing or engage in other dangerous or degrading acts. For example, at Alfred University's Alpine House, heavy alcohol consumption was integrated as a test of manhood. So important was heavy alcohol consumption to this fraternity's subculture that members would actually photograph each other vomiting. In these pictures, one can observe the sheer joy of the members watching other members get sick over the fraternity house porch railing (Nuwer 1990). Alpine House, while an extreme case, is consistent with other Greek organizations that promote higher levels of alcohol consumption than their non-Greek peers (Wechsler 1996).

It is in this social context that Alfred University freshman pledge Chuck Stenzel died from alcohol poisoning. While not forced to drink, it was clear that Chuck was pledging in a context where considerable social pressure was put on pledges to consume alcohol in excessive quantities. The individual who conforms to this type of expectation would have also experienced congratulations on being "a party animal" and receive the praise and adulation of fellow pledges and fraternity members. Court records of hazing events document that pledges who resist fraternity members' commands to drink are met with teasing and ridicule (Curry 1989). Bini Oja experienced very similar responses from the Theta Chi fraternity brothers. As he and the other pledges chugged liquor, they were accorded praise from the brothers. As members vomited, the brothers cheered. Not incidentally, the first pledge to vomit was also given a T-shirt. Obviously, the reward of a T-shirt is not sufficient motivation to behave as Bini did. The inflated sense of self created through association, however, can have a great power to influence an individual's decision to conform in situations that they would normally perceive as aversive.

Cooley's concept of the looking-glass self offers further insight into the behavior of pledges. Why would pledges agree to do something that they ordinarily would resist? According to Cooley's theory, they do so in part because they strongly desire the affirmation of others. In a context where individuals are isolated to social relations within one group, the perceived opinions of that group will take on a high level of importance in shaping a person's sense of self and their behavior in questionable circumstances.

Role Taking and the Objectified Self

James, Cooley, and Thomas offered new and interesting ways of understanding the sources of an individual's self-concept, perceptions, and reactions to situations. Their insights offer a means of understanding why pledges submit to abuse during initiation rites. If this were as far as the symbolic interactionist perspective developed, however, it would lack an explanation for one of the most fundamental questions of social psychology, the concern of how interaction is initiated and sustained. Critical readers may have accurately perceived that, thus far, I have portrayed pledges as passive recipients of circumstances, responding to events in accordance with their perceptions. What I have largely neglected is the role that pledges and fraternity members play in determining their own actions. The insights offered by George Herbert Mead (1934), in *Mind, Self and Society*, offer a means of understanding the processes by which interactions such as this are initiated and maintained.

Mead sought to develop a theory that explained the process by which two or more individuals could get together and interact in meaningful ways. For example, how do pledges and fraternity brothers initiate their relationships and maintain their associations over time? Mead's answer focused on the cognitive abilities of people to think ahead about their own actions and the actions of others. He suggested that once an individual knows how to anticipate the actions of another person, he or she can then control their own behavior to produce the reaction they desire. Mead's explanation centered on two concepts, **role taking** and the **objectification of the self.** Role taking is the mental act of viewing oneself from the position of another person. Cooley hints at this in his concept of the looking-glass self, but Mead shifts the analysis in an important way. Mead adds an emphasis on the capacity of individuals to manipulate symbolic representations of themselves and others. By creating these representations, people treat their selves as objects, things that can be manipulated at will.

To help understand the importance of his insight, imagine how your closest friend would respond if you gave him or her an expensive gold watch. Now imagine his or her reaction if you said that you stole the watch from a jewelry store. Of course it would be impossible to know exactly how your friend would respond, but you probably have a pretty good idea of whether they will think positively or negatively about you, and that their response will be in accordance with the gesture that you make toward them. In order to accomplish this task, you had to do two things simultaneously. First, you had to objectify yourself as a thing doing some potential action. Then you had to role take and assume the perspective of your friend toward the objectified self that you mentally created. Not only did you do this for one scenario, but you immediately were able to reconstruct the scenario in a very different way.

Mead argues that this ability to role take and objectify the self is a skill that people develop as they mature. Young children have only the most rudimentary skills to view themselves from the perspective of another person. However, as children mature and develop language skills, they learn to manipulate potential scenarios in their imagination. By the time children reach 4 years of age, they can think of their self in relation to their **significant others,** such as their mother, father, brother, or sister. The young child, for instance, knows (in advance) to hide the fact that he has stolen candy because he can anticipate what would happen if his mother discovered this misdeed. Mead refers to this as the **play stage** of development, which lasts roughly until the child is 6 or 7 years old. While children in the play stage can role take in relation to significant others, they are still limited in their capabilities. As evidence of these limitations, Mead points out that young children can not effectively play baseball because they are incapable of envisioning the potential actions of multiple others at the same time (such as the simultaneous actions of the runner and the basemen). They also are very poor at envisioning the consequences of their actions in relation to people that they have not met. For example, young children sometimes speak loudly of a stranger's physical deformity (much to their parents' chagrin) and have to be reminded to speak softly.

As children mature, they gain increasing sophistication in role taking and enter into what Mead referred to as the **game stage.** One advantage older children have is that they develop an understanding of what Mead terms the **generalized other.** This is a mental construct that enables a person to gauge how another typical person would respond in any particular circumstance. When people have an understanding of the generalized other, they can enter into entirely new situations and have a pretty good idea of the likely consequences of their actions. Being able to manipulate the generalized other also enables individuals to envision the actions of multiple people simultaneously. Imagine, for instance, how many individual actions a shortstop has to envision in order to execute a triple play in baseball.

Tamatsu Shibutani (1961) draws upon Mead's concept of role taking to highlight the importance of **reference groups.** Reference groups are subdivisions of society that an individual belongs to or desires to belong to, or can comprise social groupings identified by race, class, or gender, or any other socially constructed division of society. In each case, the individual thinks about how his or her actions would be viewed from the perspective of that specific subgroup of society. Rather than thinking of the perspective of society as a whole (game stage), or from the perspective of a known person (play stage), reference groups comprise a much more specific grouping of individuals. Shibutani suggested that thinking of one's self in relationship to reference groups is the most advanced form of role taking, and is characteristic of adult interaction in the **reference group stage.** As evidence of adults shifting their role taking to reference groups, consider that adolescents are often concerned with "what everybody thinks of me" and are easily embarrassed even in front of complete strangers. Adults, however, are more difficult to embarrass. In part, this is because adults define themselves more in relationship to reference groups than do adolescents. A seasoned college professor, for instance, may pay very little attention to what students think of her, but will be highly attentive to what her colleagues think. This is because students are not included in her reference group, but her colleagues are.

One thing stands clear in the analysis of fraternity hazing deaths, as well as pledging as a whole: the importance of the fraternity members as a reference group to pledges. When pledges are asked to do embarrassing or sometimes dangerous things, it is apparent that they are usually not thinking "what would my mother or father say" or "what do those strangers think of me." They are more concerned with how they might look to their fellow pledges and the fraternity members. The case of Bini Oja reveals the power of reference groups and role taking. One of Bini's fellow pledges reported in a police statement "[Bini] seemed to be drinking more than the others and I think he wanted to impress others that he could drink a lot." The pledge was probably accurate in his appraisal of Bini's motives. Bini was concerned with how this group would evaluate him. Rather than just waiting for approval to emerge, Bini willing engaged in his own hazing in anticipation of drawing social approval from the people whose opinions he valued so highly.

Members of fraternities sometimes obtain tattoos to display the organization's insignia on their body, as was the case with an entire pledge class for a fraternity at the University of Vermont. Some members of fraternities even brand fraternity letters on their forearms. The process of branding and tattooing is a symbolic display, not only of having the letters but of being willing to endure intense pain for the organization. In all probability the individuals choose to do this because they believe that it will increase their status in the group.

As previously mentioned, initiates and new members of sororities surround themselves with symbols, particularly clothing, that demonstrate their commitment to the sorority. One can see the power of reference groups in clothing choices. Interestingly, as sorority sisters approach graduation from college, they use these symbols less frequently. Rather than buying more sorority sweaters or jackets, they buy clothing more appropriate to their future professional lives. In part this is because their reference groups are shifting to potential employers and employed adults, and away from their sorority sisters (Arthur 1997).

Another aspect of Mead's theory bears emphasizing. Mead conceptualizes "the self" not as a thing, but rather as a process. People think of their selves as objects, but those objects are highly malleable and individuals are active in shaping the self that they call their own. For example, most people give considerable thought before changing their hairstyle. Although people think of their self as a stable thing, there is great potential for them to change if they want to redefine their identities. The stability of the self is largely a product of maintaining stable sets of social relations and a stable definition of what one's self is. If the relations are reshaped, or the self is redefined, the self will be reshaped as well. As an illustration, consider the profound change that occurs in people when they undergo a religious conversion such as becoming "born again" and start interacting with other people who define their selves in a like manner. A similar change occurs once individuals define themselves as "pledges" and "fraternity members."

Discussion: Sociologically Informed Strategies to Counter Fraternity Hazing

The symbolic interactionist perspective reveals that hazing is not simply the result of psychologically or morally flawed individuals; it is the result of a confluence of symbols, manipulated identities, and definitions of situations that are organized in the context of fraternity initiation rites. Eliminating fraternity hazing is a challenging proposition because it is so strongly embedded in the subculture of some fraternity houses. The symbolic interactionist perspective offers alternate understandings of pledges' and fraternity brothers' actions and leads to very different approaches in comparison to some "commonsense" solutions.

As point of contrast, consider the approach to countering fraternity hazing as informed by psychologically oriented behaviorist theory. Behaviorist theory, posits that most behavior is learned through a combination of rewards and punishments. Behaviorists assert that the likelihood of a person doing an action increases when they have already experienced a reward for that action. Conversely, one can decrease the likelihood of a person doing something in the future by according a punishment to that action. Policy implications of this theory suggest that rewarding fraternity members for desirable behaviors and punishing them for undesirable behaviors would decrease the incidence of hazing. Unfortunately, a variety of experiments reveal that rewards and punishments do not always work as one would expect (Kohn 1993).

In the case of fraternities and hazing, it is not unusual for problematic fraternities to have been punished in the past for rule transgressions. This was the case with Alpine House prior to the hazing death of Chuck Stenzel at Alfred University (Nuwer 1990). It was also the case at Stetson University, where members of the Chi chapter were expelled for shocking pledges with an electrical device. Nonetheless, the fraternity continued to use electrical shocks in their initiation rites (Nuwer 1990; 303). Using fiction as an illustrator, some may recall the film *Animal House,* wherein the fraternity brothers responded to the dean's punishment of "double secret probation" by having a party. It is quite clear that punishments only work if the punished party perceives the punishment as warranted. If this condition is not satisfied, punishment only serves to build hostility between the authority figure and the punished individual, and to drive problematic behavior further underground.

In contrast, symbolic interactionists suggest that reform hinges on the examination of meaning systems. Because individuals respond to the world in accordance with the definitions they hold, it is the definitions that need shifting, not so much the rewards and punishments. Fraternity hazing results from definitions of situations that compel fraternity members to believe that abuse of recruits is a necessary part of entry into the fraternity. In fact, Greek organizations use the same type of strategy other groups use to cultivate strong commitment and loyalty (Leemon 1972). Doctors, for instance, are commonly hazed (although this term is not used) during residency, when they are expected to work incredibly long shifts that necessarily involve sleep deprivation (Becker, Geer, Hughes, and Straus 1961). As discussed above, hazing occurs because fraternities define it as a necessary part of their initiation rites and package it carefully to pledges so as to produce compliance.

Pledges and fraternity members are susceptible to losing perspective on what constitutes a reasonable expectation during pledging rites. Friends and teachers outside of fraternities and sororities, however, may be able to identify problems in the initiation rites and offer some means of redefining situations. For example, a couple of years ago a young woman came into one of my classes with a large paper clock tied around her neck. On the clock was written the phrase "ask me what time it is." The student's head repeatedly dropped during the class and she obviously was struggling to keep her eyes open. At the end of class, I tactfully asked her to stay behind for a moment. With the other students gone, I told her that I knew she was being asked to stay awake by her sorority sisters. She did not deny this. I told her that I didn't expect her to break her vow of secrecy, but that I wanted her to recognize that she was being hazed. She responded that "it would be all over soon." I responded again, "I want you to recognize that you are being hazed." From her nonverbal response, I saw that this registered and a new reality was created. I then followed this statement by saying "I want you to recognize that right now it is a choice for you to submit to this abuse and that you can choose to go to sleep if you want to." This interaction only took about five minutes and demonstrated that definitions of situations can be changed.

Hazing is embedded in Greek culture, and changing a culture is not an easy matter. Studies reveal that Greek culture places a high value on secrecy and autonomy (Leemon 1972). This aspect of Greek society is especially problematic for college authorities, who are likely perceived as "outsiders," and as a consequence have few opportunities to learn about the positive and negative things that occur in fraternities. Fraternities are also not receptive to intrusion into what they perceive as internal affairs. Because college authorities do not constitute a salient reference group for Greek members, well-intentioned advice from advisors or administrators can go unheeded.

Given that college authorities are not a reference group, one possible approach to countering fraternity hazing is to use groups that will be accorded immediate respect by fraternities. National fraternity organization representatives are one such group, and can offer reflections and advice that would otherwise not be well received. There may be a very different reaction, for example, to an instructional program on safe use of alcohol during pledging if it is presented by the student life administrator or if it is presented by an alumnus with a Greek affiliation.

Another possibility is to dramatize the potential consequences of hazing. This approach has been used by the Committee to Halt Useless College Killings (CHUCK) (Gose 1997; Nuwer 1990). CHUCK was founded in 1978 by

Eileen Stevens, following the death of her son in a fraternity hazing incident. Rather than college authorities laying down rules of what can and cannot be done in initiations, Eileen Stevens comes to fraternities as an outsider and organizes dramatic representations of what happens following a hazing death. One especially effective means of teaching these lessons involves a mock courtroom, where members of the fraternity are expected to take the stand in defense of a hypothetical pledging rite that resulted in a pledge's death at their fraternity.

Another direct application of symbolic interactionism relates to the insight of the social nature of the self. The symbolic interactionist perspective reveals that pledges' willingness to submit to abuse is linked with their inability to think of themselves outside of their status as future fraternity members. Pledges literally lose their "old self" during the pledging process, as they are given new identity kits, social relations, and definitions of self and are shifted to a new reference group. As pledges construct new identities to correspond with fraternity membership, they have greater difficulties envisioning alternate paths of action that contradict the desires of their reference group. Left unchecked, fraternities and sororities will likely exploit the advantages of socially isolating their pledges. Although this will not necessarily lead to hazing, it increases the likelihood that pledges will submit to being hazed.

Advisors and administrators can curtail this potential by limiting the power of fraternities and sororities to isolate pledges from other social groups. Student affairs professionals can help prevent hazing by structuring policies to maintain pledges' connections with other students outside of the Greek subculture. For example, following a recent hazing death, the Massachusetts Institute of Technology now restricts pledging to students who have already completed their freshman year. Possibly this policy will enable new students to build stronger relationships outside of fraternities, thereby making resistance to hazing a more tenable alternative.

Social problems such as fraternity hazing have no easy solutions. Symbolic interactionism offers some useful insights, though, in explaining this problematic social behavior. Maintaining sensitivity to the ways in which fraternities understand hazing, and the ways fraternities shape pledges' abilities to define their selves, may be the best way to construct programs and policies to prevent hazing.

REFERENCES

Adler, Patricia and Peter Adler. 1989. "The Glorified Self." *Social Psychology Quarterly.* 52:299–310.

Arthur, Linda Boynton. 1997. "Role Salience, Role Embracement, and the Symbolic Self Completion of Sorority pledges." *Sociological Inquiry.* 67:364–379.

Becker, Howard, B. Geer, E. C. Hughes & A. Straus. 1961. *The Boys in White: Student Culture in the Medical World*. Chicago: University of Chicago Press.

Blumer, Herbert. 1969. *Symbolic Interactionism: Perspective and Method*. Englewood Cliffs, NJ: Prentice Hall.

Cooley, Charles Horton. 1970. *Human Nature and the Social Order*. New York: Schocken Books.

Coser, Lewis. 1974. *Greedy Institutions: Patterns of Undivided Commitment*. New York: Free Press.

Curry, Susan. 1989. "Hazing and the 'Rush' Toward Reform: Responses from Universities, Fraternities, State Legislatures, and the Courts." *Journal of College and University Law*. 16:93–117.

Goffman, Erving. 1959. *The Presentation of Self in Everyday Life*. New York: Anchor.

Goffman, Erving. 1961. *Asylums*. Chicago: Aldine.

Gose, Ben. 1997. "Efforts to End Fraternity Hazing Have Largely Failed, Critics Charge." *Chronicle of Higher Education*. April 18: pp. A37, A38.

James, William. 1983. *The Principles of Psychology*. Cambridge, MA: Harvard University Press.

Katz, F. 1993. *Ordinary People and Extraordinary Evil: A Report on the Beguilings of Evil*. Albany, NY: SUNY Press.

Kohn, Alfie. 1993. *Punished by Rewards*. New York: Houghton Mifflin.

Lakoff, George & Mark Johnson. 1980. *Metaphors We Live By*. Chicago: University of Chicago Press.

Leemon, Thomas. 1972. *Rites of Passage in a Student Culture*. New York: Teachers College.

Martin, Patricia Yancey and Robert Hummer. 1989. "Fraternities and Rape on Campus." *Gender and Society*. 3:457–473.

Mead, George Herbert. 1934. *Mind, Self, and Society*. Chicago: University of Chicago Press.

Moffatt, Michael. 1989. *Coming of Age in New Jersey*. New Brunswick, NJ: Rutgers University Press.

Nurius, Paula, Jeanette Norris, Linda Dimeff, and Thomas Graham. 1996. "Expectations Regarding Acquaintance Sexual Aggression Among Sorority and Fraternity Members." *Sex Roles*. 35:427–444.

Nuwer, Hank. 1990. *Broken Pledges: The Deadly Rite of Hazing*. Atlanta: Longstreet Press.

Rhoads, Robert. 1995. "Whale Tales, Dog Piles, and Beer Goggles: An Ethnographic Case Study of Fraternity Life." *Anthropology and Education Quarterly*. 26:306–323.

Sanday, Peggy Reeves. 1990. *Fraternity Gang Rape: Sex, Brotherhood, and Privilege on Campus*. New York: New York University Press.

Shaw, Deborah Lee & Thomas Morgan. 1990. "Greek Advisor's Perceptions of Sorority Hazing." *NASPA Journal*. 28:60–64.

Shibutani, Tamatsu. 1961. *Society and Personality: An Interactionist Approach to Social Psychology*. Englewood Cliffs, NJ: Prentice Hall.

Snow, David and Leon Anderson. 1993. *Salvaging the Self from Homelessness. Down on Their Luck: A Study of Homeless Street People*. Berkeley: University of California Press.

Strombler, Mary. 1994. "'Buddies' or 'Slutties': The Collective Sexual Reputation of Fraternity Little Sisters." *Gender & Society*. 8:297–323.

Thomas, W. I. 1928. *The Child in America*. Chicago: University of Chicago Press.

U.S. Government Accounting Office. 1992. *DOD Service Academies: More Changes Needed to Eliminate Hazing*. Washington, D.C.: GAO/NSIAD-93-36.

van Gennep, Arnold. 1960 [1909]. *The Rites of Passage*, translated by Monika Vizedom and Gabrielle Caffee. Chicago: University of Chicago Press.

Wechsler, Henry. 1996. "Alcohol and the American College Campus: A Report from the Harvard School of Public Health. *Change*. 28:20–25.

Zimbardo, P. G. 1972. "Pathology of Imprisonment." *Transaction/Society* 9:4–8.

3 Gender, Inequality, and College Society

In May 1999, the Massachusetts Institute of Technology released *A Study on the Status of Women Faculty in Science at MIT.* This study provides an interesting glimpse into the experiences of women faculty at one of the most prestigious universities in the world—a vision that is not altogether rosy. Of the 266 faculty in MIT's School of Science, only 31 were women, and fewer still were tenured. Dissatisfaction among these women was high, particularly among the senior women faculty who had witnessed a variety of circumstances in which men were given preferential treatment. Being small in number, it was difficult for these women to find patterns in these experiences, but some data were telling. Confidential analyses of faculty salaries in 1994 revealed that women faculty at MIT were earning considerably less than their male counterparts. To redress this issue, the Dean of the School of Science raised their salaries by 20 percent, but other problems persisted. In comparison to men, the average woman faculty member at MIT had less than half the space (a precious commodity at a research institution), fewer resources, and fewer opportunities than men to be included in positions of power. In fact, all of the top administrators at MIT were men. One of the most surprising findings of this report was that many employees at the university, some of the women included, did not know that discrimination was occurring. Rather than seeing pervasive patterns signifying these problems, the tendency was to attribute the experiences of individual women to "special circumstances."

The MIT report opens as many questions as it answers. For instance, are the problems unique to MIT, or do they signify a more pervasive problem that extends into other institutions of higher education? If it is a pervasive problem, what factors can explain why there are so few women faculty represented in science departments, so few in tenured positions, or so few in positions of power in administration? Furthermore, if this is the case, what policies should institutions like MIT construct to remedy the problem?

These questions emanate from one of the most important sociological concerns, the study of power and inequality in society. This chapter reveals striking parallels between the types of gender inequality on campus and gender inequality in society. For instance, although white males comprise only 33% of the U.S. population in the mid 1990s, they constituted 85% of partners in law firms, 80% of the House of Representatives, 90% of the U.S. Senate, and 95% of Fortune 500 chief executive officers (Benokraitis 1997). Women still only earn, on average, about 75 cents for every dollar men earn (Rhode 1997). Despite these facts, most Americans continue to think that opportunities for success are generally distributed in a fair manner and only one in four American women state that they are very concerned about gender inequality (Rhode 1997).

In this chapter, I adopt a feminist perspective in the study of gender inequality on campus. There are some problems with the term "feminism," though, that warrant consideration before inequality on campus and society is examined in further detail. First, feminism is a hot-button term that implies, for many, an extremist position (i.e., Rush Limbaugh's term "femi-nazis") and is frequently equated with simply meaning "man hating" (Rhode 1997). Although feminists have worked for years to advance the interests of women, it is interesting that young women are especially reluctant to call themselves "feminists" (Lorber 1994). At the same time, most young women are quick to say that they believe that they are every bit a man's equal and that they should have the same rights as men (an orientation of the feminist perspective).

Also, there is no single, agreed-upon definition of what constitutes a feminist perspective, or who is, or is not, a feminist. Despite disagreements among feminists, and even the unwillingness of some feminists to call themselves such, women and men adopting this perspective share much in common. First, feminists believe that it is necessary to study gender to fully comprehend society. There are important differences between the ways in which men and women are treated in society, and these differences need to be examined before one can fully understand social relations. Second, feminists believe that many of the differences between men and women are socially imposed. While there may be some biological causes for some differences between men and women, most observable differences are created through enduring cultural practices and are not simply the result of genetics. Third, feminists focus on the ways in which women are disadvantaged in society. Toward this end, there is an inclination to view current forms of social relations skeptically, and to think critically about processes that offer advantages to men in the social system. Fourth, feminists also reveal the unique contributions women make to society, calling attention to the ways in which these activities are frequently undervalued. Fifth, feminists believe that the current social order can be changed to advance the interests of women. In this way, feminism is as much a political movement as it is an intellectual orientation (see Lorber 1994; Rhode 1997). This orientation helps to create a theoretically informed understanding of the social mechanisms that create gender inequality on campus and in society as a whole, as well as creating policies to help remedy these problems.

Gender in a Stratified Society

Stratification is a term sociologists use to describe the layering of society into levels of social hierarchy that confer social status, power, or economic reward. Commonly these levels reveal varying concentrations of different types of people. Sometimes, though, the importance of stratification is cloaked by an apparent proportionate distribution of people within organizations. For example, over half of the employees in colleges and universities are women. However, as Figure 3.1 reveals, when analyzed in terms of their location in the stratified college society, women are disproportionately located at the lowest levels of the social hierarchy, in the strata of nonprofessional service, maintenance, secretarial, and clerical workers. On the other hand, men are more heavily concentrated in the economically rewarding and prestigious positions such as faculty and administrators. The high participation of women in college society, and the wider economy, may be one reason why most Americans do not perceive gender inequality as a major social problem.

A person's location within a stratification system can have a profound impact on his or her movement within that system. **Social mobility** describes the movement of a person from one level in the stratification system to a higher or lower level. In **caste societies,** such as premodern India, social mobility was greatly restricted because one's position was ascribed at birth. In **class societies,** such as present-day America, even though adult roles are not ascribed at birth, the position a person occupies in the economy has a great influence on his/her potential of achieving upward mobility. The fact that women are disproportionately employed in nonprofessional jobs is extremely important to consider because this class position poses very real barriers to their social mobility.

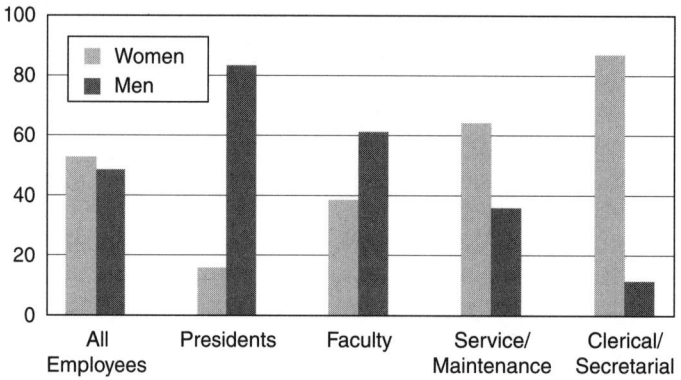

FIGURE 3.1   College Employees by Gender Percentages 1993

Source: Chronicle of Higher Education 1995

Women working in professional jobs receive relatively good incomes, job security, and benefits in comparison to women working in nonprofessional jobs. For women laboring in professional positions, their concern has historically been to break through the **glass ceiling,** the invisible barrier to achieving the highest levels of accomplishment (Kanter 1977). On the other hand, a major problem facing nonprofessional women is the **sticky floor** (Reskin and Padavic 1994). Because workers laboring in secretarial and service positions gain only limited new skills on the job, they experience fewer opportunities to propel themselves into positions that offer greater status and financial reward. For many women, this means lifelong careers in jobs that offer few chances for advancement.

One of the most daunting problems for women on campus is similar to a major problem facing women in the wider economy. The single biggest explanatory factor for women's low wages is that women are funneled into the types of jobs that pay lower salaries (Lorber 1994; Peterson and Morgan 1995). Because greater proportions of women labor in low-paying nonprofessional jobs, as a group women earn far less than men. Like women in the larger economy, female college employees are more likely to be employed in part-time jobs and in positions that offer fewer chances for advancement. Until gender ratios shift, with more women working in professional jobs, women will continue earning much less than men, on and off campus (Peterson and Morgan 1995). Clearly, women are not faring as well as men in the wider economy or on college campuses.

The distinction of the glass ceiling from the sticky floor highlights the need to consider social class in understanding the constraints and barriers facing women in society. In some respects, the experiences of middle-class women and lower-class women are similar. For example, in both classes, women are responsible for the majority of childrearing responsibilities. However, middle-class women have many advantages that are not open to lower-class women. Studies of women in poverty, such as Stack's (1997) *All Our Kin,* show that lower-class women live in structural and cultural conditions that make their lives distinct from middle-class women. For example, in contrast to middle-class women, lower-class women have to work in order to contribute money to the family economy. In contrast, for middle-class women the decision to pursue a career and a family is to a greater extent a choice, rather than an economic imperative. Also, the types of jobs that middle-class women pursue offer many advantages that are unavailable to lower-class women. These jobs offer higher social status, as well as important economic benefits such as access to health insurance and greater job security.

These observations make clear the need to study the constraints facing women as influenced by both class and gender. In addition, other factors such as ethnicity, age, disability, and sexual orientation influence men's and women's lives in different ways. In this chapter, I focus primarily on the experiences of middle-class women, both students and faculty, to highlight the insights offered by a feminist perspective. This same perspective, and many of the analytic strategies, can also be used to understand the experiences of lower-class women.

Nonsociological explanations of gender inequality among both lower-class and middle-class women often involve examining individual women for the sources of their comparative failure in the economy. For example, a psychologist may strive to find out whether women suffer from some type of personality disorder or shortcoming such as a "fear of success" or a lack of self-esteem. The feminist perspective suggests an alternative way of framing the concerns. If women are not inherently different from men, women must have the potential to be as successful as men. If this is the case, the concern shifts to identifying the types of social barriers to this potential success. Feminist inquiry has traditionally focused on two overarching explanations for the persistence of these barriers: socialization and discrimination.

Socialization and Gender Inequality

When sociologists discuss differences between men and women, they distinguish sex from gender. A person's sex is genetically determined. For males, sex determines such important things as having a penis and the ability to grow ear hair. For women, sex determines the ability to become pregnant and lactate. Gender, however, is socially constructed and encompasses the expectations of men and women that are not linked to biology. Sex, for example, determines that women can nurse children. Gender, however, determines that women assume the majority of childcare responsibilities in a family.

When a difference is **socially constructed,** it means that this difference can be attributed to social factors outside of some type of unchangeable genetic predisposition. An example may help illuminate this concern. Consider the very real differences between black slaves and white slave owners in nineteenth-century America. For the slave owner, the "facts" plainly showed that the Negro race was intellectually inferior to white people of European ancestry. For the white slave owner, the proof of the inherent (biological) social inferiority of the slave was self-evident. Modern sensibilities lead to very different interpretations of the differences between slave owners and the slaves: the differences were not biologically caused, they were produced through the socially constructed practice of slavery itself, which stipulated that slaves not attend schools or be allowed to become literate. The social construction of a difference between blacks and whites was so effectively instilled that white slave owners were oblivious to the pervasive similarities between themselves and their slaves.

The theory of a social construction of gender centers on a very similar arrangement. There are major differences between men and women in society, but these differences are largely the product of a shared agreement that men and women need to be distinguished from one another (Beall 1993). So imbedded is the cultural practice of distinguishing males from females that it is difficult to refer to individuals without revealing their gender through the use of symbols such as "he" or "she." Modern social conventions establish differences between men and women, rather than commonalities. Because people operate on these beliefs, these differences are reproduced systematically and are reified.

Throughout their lives, men and women receive signals from other people of how society is supposed to operate and their position in that social order. These lessons are learned through **socialization,** the process though which people gain an understanding of their roles in society in relation to everyone else (Charon 1995). In some circumstances these signals are so overt and structured that they are considered **formal socialization.** For instance, children are instructed to raise their hands before speaking in class and to say thank you when receiving a gift (Cahill 1987). Similarly, boys learn that "big boys don't cry," and misbehaving girls are instructed to "act like a lady." Most learning of gender roles occurs, however, through **informal socialization,** subtle gestures or cues that other people send to boys and girls to behave in accordance with their gender roles. Eye contact, words of reassurance, and attention all play a role in encouraging people to continue pursuing an activity or goal. On the other hand, avoidance of eye contact or skeptical comments operate to discourage individuals. Young boys and girls receive such signals when they act outside of customary gender role expectations.

There are a variety of **agents of socialization** that teach people to conform to these social expectations. The three most important agents of socialization are primary groups, secondary groups, and the mass media. **Primary groups** are people with whom individuals have close personal relationships, such as family and friends. Because these relations are so intimate, they have tremendous power in defining a person's understanding of him/herself. Parents, for instance, engage in very different forms of contact between infant boys and girls, socializing them at a very early age to have different levels of independence (Lott and Mauls 1993). Parents typically buy gendered toys, for example, selecting trucks for boys and dolls for girls. Fathers and mothers also serve as role models for children, and push children to aspire to behave in ways that are similar to their same- sex parent (Chodorow 1978).

Secondary groups are people with whom individuals have face-to-face relationships, but these relationships are of a less personal nature and often are of shorter duration. Although these relationships are less intimate than primary groups, they can have a strong influence on a person's aspirations. Members of secondary groups, such as teachers and guidance counselors, play a major role in shaping children's aspirations to conform with gender roles. A widely cited report by the American Association of University Women, *How*

Schools Shortchange Girls (1992), details a variety of school practices that dissuade girls from entering into male-oriented careers. One way in which schools influence girls' aspirations is by modeling the gendered hierarchy of the workplace. For example, in 1990, 72% of principals and 95% of superintendents were male. In comparison, the overwhelming majority of all elementary school teachers are female (National Center for Education Statistics 1996). As a consequence, students learn to associate gender with occupation and place their aspirations according to what seems appropriate to their gender. Another way in which gender is socialized through schools is the different interactions counselors have with boy and girl students. While not nearly as problematic as it was in earlier decades, these agents of socialization still tend to advise students to enter into jobs conforming to traditional sex roles. As evidence of the failure of schools to equally shape boys' and girls' aspirations, the AAUW (1992) reports that in 1990 were high school boys were four times more likely to aspire to a career in engineering than girls were, and twice as likely to aspire to a career in computer science. Girls were much more inclined to express intents to pursue careers in social science and teaching.

A third major force in socialization is the **mass media.** Even though most people do not have face-to-face encounters with writers, editors, or celebrities, these people influence lives in profound ways by producing newspaper, magazine, Internet, and television accounts of what is appropriate behavior for males and females. Saturday morning television commercials, for instance, show boys and girls playing in accordance with traditional sex roles. Adults are not immune to the influence of the mass media either. Seldom, for example, do commercials show men engaging in housework. In *The Way We Never Were* (1992) Stephanie Coontz reveals that adults often use fictional images of life-as-presented-on-television (bearing little resemblance to reality) as their guide to what to expect from their spouses, children, and other members of society.

Because people internalize social expectations of gender roles, socialization directly affects career aspirations. Data concerning college students' choices of majors indicate continued relevance of the types of differential socialization, as shown in Figure 3.2. In 1994, women comprised over one-half (54%) of the graduates receiving bachelor's degrees. Female undergraduates were much more likely than men to major in the health professions (predominantly nursing), education, psychology, visual arts, and communications. Men, on the other hand, constituted three-fourths of those majoring in computer science and five-sixths of the engineering majors (National Center for Education Statistics 1996). Hundreds of studies affirm that people are socialized to have very different expectations of what women do and what men do (see Lorber 1994; Valian 1998). This, in part, can help explain why women are underrepresented among science faculty and among college administrators. Even if equal opportunity currently exists for women to enter these profes-

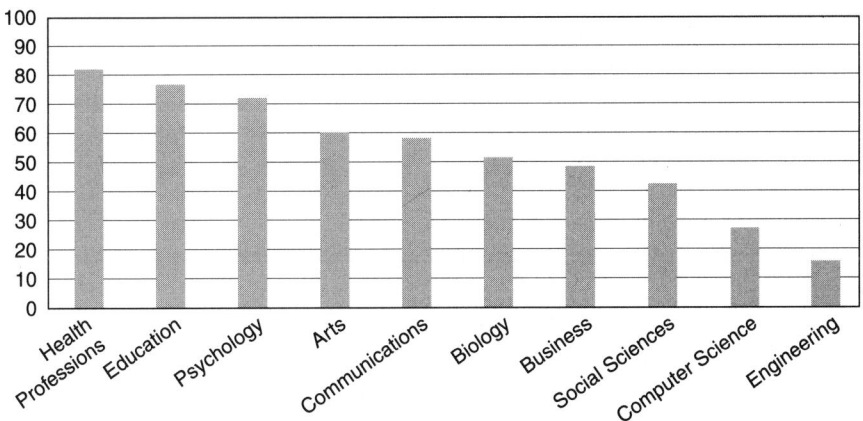

FIGURE 3.2   Percent of Bachelor's Degrees Conferred to Women 1993–94
Source: U.S. Dept. of Education 1996

sions, subtle and not so subtle social pressures exerted on girls can sway them toward traditional gender roles and away from historically male-dominated professions.

Some studies suggest that these pressures may be lessening. One such study, *Women, Minorities, and Persons with Disabilities in Science and Engineering 1998* (National Science Foundation 1999), offers an optimistic portrayal of the state of preparedness of young women to enter the sciences. In contrast with earlier generations, high school girls are now taking advanced math and science courses at about the same frequency as high school boys, and their attainment in these courses is nearly the same. Although women attaining doctoral degrees in the sciences are still in the minority, the proportion of women receiving these degrees increased from 26% of the total number of degrees conferred in 1985 to 31% in 1995. This study suggests that aspirations may account for some of the differences between men and women; it also suggests that disparity in the aspirations between men and women is shrinking. Even so, it is important to recognize that two-thirds of the doctoral degrees in the sciences are being received by men.

Gender Role Conflicts

Socialization can produce **gender-role conflicts.** A role conflict emerges when competing demands are placed upon a person, making it difficult to satisfy all of the expectations associated with the responsibilities associated with these roles. Feminist theory suggests that women are more likely to experience gender role conflicts because of the myriad demands that require straddling job and child-rearing responsibilities.

Traditional sex roles mandate that men be the breadwinners in a family and women perform housework and childcare. These roles have shifted in the past three decades, with increasing proportions of women working full-time outside of the home, producing new opportunities, as well as new problems for women and families. One telling statistic is that in 1997 nearly two-thirds (60%) of married mothers with a child under age 1 were in the workforce (U.S. Bureau of the Census 1997).

In *The Second Shift*, Arlie Hochschild (1989) details the experiences of women who attempt to pursue careers and families. While women have entered successful careers, Hochschild found that their integration into the workforce has not excused them from the traditional gender role responsibilities of cooking, cleaning, and childcare. Men experience considerable stress in satisfying work and family demands as well, but according to Juliet Schor's (1991) study *The Overworked American*, there is an important difference between men and women and where they focus their energies. According to this study, men and women perform approximately equal amounts of combined housework and paid work. However, in comparing the amount of time spent in paid work and the amount of time spent in housework, Schor reveals that men tend to work more hours at the office, and women tend to put in more hours in the home. At the end of a year, the average woman performed 434 more hours of housework compared with men. Likewise, the average man performed 441 more hours of paid work compared with women.

The responsibility for housework and childcare has a direct impact on women's productivity in the paid labor force. Some indicators suggest that men, as a group, may be more productive on the job than women. For example, studies show that male faculty publish articles at about twice the rate of female faculty (Valian 1998). Also, according to data compiled by the National Research Council (National Center for Education Statistics 1996), in 1993 men pursuing doctorates, on average, received their degree 8 years following the completion of a bachelor's degree, whereas it took women, on average, 11 years. Gender role conflicts can probably account for much of these differences, as childcare and household maintenance absorb considerable portions of women's time.

Many middle-class women have to make thorny decisions of whether to concentrate on family or career. In the case of MIT, a poll of women faculty found that their most common concern was the difficulty of combining work and family (MIT 1999). According to Hochschild (1989), some women attempt to resolve this conflict by sacrificing sleep and personal time. A study by Becker and Moen (1999) found that couples are responding to these conflicts by scaling back on career expectations and that wives are more likely to scale back than husbands. Role conflicts such as these take a heavier toll on women and, as a consequence, influence their economic and occupational attainment.

Normative Alternatives

Another aspect of the power of socialization is revealed in **normative alternatives theory.** According to Fiorentine and Cole (1992), men and women are socialized to use different yardsticks to measure their success. For women, success is measured by a number of roles, including that of mother, worker, spouse, and friend. Men, on the other hand, place much of their identity in their job and career. As a consequence of being socialized to find their identity in their career, it is comparatively more problematic for a man to be a failure at work than it is for a woman. This places greater pressure on men to succeed, and as a consequence men are possibly more perseverant in pursuing career-oriented goals than women are.

Completing graduate school, for example, is a very challenging activity. Many graduate students finish their education as "A.B.D." (all but dissertation) and never attain a Ph.D. Because female graduate students have more face-saving options in comparison with male graduate students, the option of withdrawing from school becomes more tenable, as does pursuing a graduate degree on a slower "mommy track" pace. This social pressure may also increase men's persistence in obtaining research grants, applying for jobs in the face of rejection letters, and resubmitting rejected research articles. Lacking alternative roles, men focus more heavily on their jobs and this in turn may create greater productivity.

Normative alternatives theory could be interpreted as "blaming the victim," because it suggests that women's lower achievements can be attributed to a lack of tenacity. However, I think a more accurate interpretation is that women's roles allow for exits that are sometimes not available to men. As a consequence, women can make rational choices to pursue other activities in the face of job difficulties. On the other hand, because men's individual worth is assessed by their success on the job, they lack the alternative to redirect their lives in other directions. As a consequence, some men may actually bind themselves to job success at the cost of a more well-rounded life.

With the confluence of these forces in mind, one would predict that dual career couples would tend to make choices that favor the husband's career over the wife's. I tested this assumption with data from the *1998–1999 Cornell Couples and Careers Study,* a data set that includes interviews with 239 couples who had at least one member working in one of two prestigious universities. In this survey, husbands and wives were asked to think about all the major decisions that they and their spouses have made since they have been together, such as changing jobs, having children, going back to school, or moving, and to consider whose career took priority. Only one-third of these couples reported that they had taken turns or that neither spouse's career took priority. Nearly half of men (44%) and women (49%) reported that the husband's career took priority. Only one in five of the women (19%) and men (17%) reported that the wife's career took priority.

Men in the *Cornell Couples and Careers Study* also reported having more opportunities to advance themselves either through career or education that would have required their spouse to make significant changes in her life. Nearly half of the men working at the universities (46%) report having such an opportunity, whereas only one-quarter of the women (24%) report likewise. Furthermore, of those who had these opportunities, nearly half of the women (47%) turned them down. Only one-third of the men (36%) responded likewise. Taken together, these findings indicate that women in college society are less inclined to pursue opportunities that will require their husbands to make changes in their lives. When the opportunities do present themselves, women are also less likely to follow these opportunities in comparison to their husbands.

Can the Forces of Gender Socialization Be Countered?

One step in diminishing the degree of gender inequality on college campuses, and in the wider economy, is to recognize that there are different cultural expectations for men and women. These shape aspirations and funnel women into lower-paying jobs. It is part of a process that involves differentiating women from men and binds women to housework and childcare responsibilities. These tasks, in turn, detract from women's ability to spend as many hours as men working in paid employment. It is also possible that men are socialized to be more perseverant in pursuing job-related goals, but possibly at the expense of their other relationships.

It seems apparent that eliminating gender inequality requires creating a social climate that minimizes the impact of gender roles on children's aspirations and expectations of each other. Parents, siblings, and friends often shape children's personalities so that they conform to traditional gender roles. Perhaps sociologists and educators can play a role in calling attention to the presence of these forces, making people self-aware of their actions that reinforce these roles.

Henry Giroux (1997) believes that teachers can play a powerful role in teaching children the skills to deconstruct gender stereotypes as they are presented in the mass media. To **deconstruct** is to tear a cultural product apart in order to examine the assumptions and symbols that its foundation comprises. Examining these elements, and the ways they are configured together, reveals issues of power that otherwise go unnoticed. Disney movies, for instance, can be deconstructed in the classroom in order to teach lessons on sexism, racism, classism, and ageism in the mass media. Movies such as

Cinderella, *The Little Mermaid*, and *Beauty and the Beast*, for example, all show female characters as being incomplete without a male romantic interest and thereby reinforce sexist stereotypes of women as being frail, in need of rescuing, and dependent upon men. Movies such as *Aladdin* offer equally negative portrayals of ethnic groups. Giroux argues that children are very capable of understanding the power the media has to shape attitudes, but simply lack the skills. Once these skills are developed, children are better positioned to think of themselves and others in ways that are not in accordance with these prefabricated images.

Schools have the potential to help create an atmosphere where boys and girls are liberated to explore their many capabilities, whether these capabilities conform to gender norms or not. The success of schools, though, will necessarily be linked with the degree to which other agents of socialization are sensitive to gender stereotypes. Outside of censorship, reshaping media presentations of women and men, for example, would be difficult to accomplish, and the desirability of this tactic is highly questionable. Perhaps, though, as people learn to identify the forces that shape children into boys and girls, they can personally intercede, helping to shape aspirations of their own children and those of their neighbors and friends in ways that are not dictated by traditional gender roles.

Discrimination and Gender Inequality

The above discussion has shown that some of the differences between male and female earnings and occupations can be attributed to the forces of socialization. What happens, though, when women enter into previously male dominated domains and buck gender roles? Figure 3.3 offers some telling information to suggest that their footing is anything but equal. Even after controlling for academic rank, faculty women earn on average considerably less than faculty men.

An overarching explanation for this disparity is discrimination. **Discrimination** occurs when subordinate groups (in this case women) are denied access to the types of rewards and resources open to dominant groups (Feagin and Feagin 1978). In some circumstances, discrimination results from the actions of bigoted or prejudiced individuals who deliberately try to do harm to others. Discrimination can also occur unintentionally, and people can do others harm even without intending to do so. In other circumstances discrimination is the result of the normal operating procedures of society. These unintentional and institutionalized forms of discrimination are among the most serious factors that influence gender inequality in academia and the larger society. To study the power of discrimination on campus, the remainder of this chapter focuses on three distinct types of discrimination:

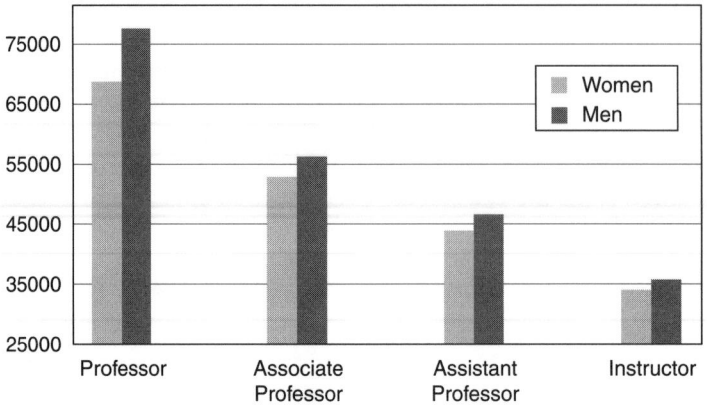

FIGURE 3.3   Average Faculty Income by Gender and Rank 1999
Source: Academe 2000

intentional discrimination, unintentional discrimination, and institutional discrimination.

Intentional Discrimination

One source of the disparity between women and men can be attributed to forms of intentional discrimination. **Intentional discrimination** occurs because members of society make decisions to deprive other members of equitable rights and privileges. In part, this may be attributed to **prejudice,** preexisting beliefs about individuals because of their membership in a particular social group. Sometimes intentional discrimination occurs because of hostility, such as in the nineteenth century when shopkeepers posted "Irish Need Not Apply" signs on their windows. Sometimes it occurs simply because dominant members take for granted that some groups should be treated differently than others. This was the case at Dartmouth University, which didn't start admitting women into its undergraduate programs until 1972.

Intentional discrimination operates on three levels (Benokraitis 1997). *Blatant sex discrimination* is the most easily recognized form of sexism because it involves overt hostile acts toward women, such as sexual harassment or clear favoritism in hiring and promotion decisions. Current law stipulates that when employees observe these abuses of power, they should have an opportunity to complain and have these injustices corrected. *Subtle sex discrimination* involves sending women messages about their lack of value to an organization. Asking professional women to take notes at meetings, treating them with kid gloves, or passing sexual jokes at the water cooler, all are examples of subtle sexism. In these circumstances, women are not denied the right to work at the organization, but they are subtly reminded that their status is lower than men's and that they are primarily valued for their traditional gender roles, not for their contributions to the job. The law is less clear on when these activities constitute discrimination, thus making response more difficult.

Still more problematic is *covert sex discrimination*. This involves men secretly plotting with one another to undermine a woman's chances on the job. Because women are not privy to these discussions, they will be unlikely to know that it is occurring. Lacking this knowledge, or evidence to establish its occurrence, victims of covert sex discrimination are usually powerless to instigate redress (Benokraitis 1997). In part, these types of intentional discrimination can explain some of the gender differentials in faculty pay.

Rosabeth Moss Kanter identified these problems in her study *Women and Men of the Corporation* (1977) and she suggested that their origin stems from the "homophilic culture of the corporation." In many organizations, colleges and universities included, the main power-holders are men who share in common masculine values. These men sometimes interpret inclusion of women as threats to their status. As a consequence, they avoid contact with women and work to promote the interests of other men. There is some merit to the argument that colleges and universities may be similar to the corporation Moss Kanter studied. In 1995, men comprised 86% of college presidents, and also comprised the vast majority of provosts, deans, and department chairs. These men tend to work and socialize together and sometimes create informal male groups termed "old boys clubs" (DeKeseredy 1990).

Old boys clubs, by virtue of being sex segregated, effectively limit women's access to valuable social networks. For example, women are largely excluded from social activities on the golf course and in the locker room. As a consequence, they are less likely to learn of the boss's big concerns or his plans before they are formally announced. They also have a lower likelihood of learning about potential job openings and therefore are less able to groom themselves for these opportunities. This implies that even if women are treated equally in formal evaluation and employment decisions, their social exclusion from informal contact with male power-holders insures that the pace of their career advancement will be slow. The existence of old boys clubs may, in part, explain why tenured faculty women at MIT reported feeling marginalized, and why they were deprived of access to space, resources, and inclusion in positions of power (MIT 1999).

One study offers a glimpse of intentional discrimination in action on a college campus and the difficulties confronting one woman subjected to a hostile work environment. Using a case study approach, Gallant and Cross (1993) examine the experiences of a new female faculty member, who they call the "newcomer." Like many other female faculty on college campuses, the newcomer found herself socially isolated from her male colleagues. She was not accepted into the old boys club or into the clique of less successful younger male colleagues in her department. She also had the unfortunate experience of being sexually propositioned by her departmental chair. The chair was a member in good standing of the university's old boys club, maintaining strong friendships with the dean and other high-status male members in other departments. Because the newcomer was socially isolated, she could not rely on other colleagues to come to her defense. As a consequence, she made a pragmatic choice to politely but firmly decline the initial sexual advance and not to make an issue of it. The chair persisted with further propositions, making the workplace extremely uncomfortable. As a consequence, the newcomer not only had to concentrate on how to do her job, but also how to avoid the chair and how to respond when avoidance was impossible.

As these problems persisted, the newcomer started having sleepless nights and felt considerable stress on the job. Feeling rejected, the chair became hostile and assigned the newcomer a greater share of menial departmental work. These assignments were likely intended as retribution and the newcomer was forced to comply because of her status as a junior faculty member. The chair also spread rumors concerning the newcomer's teaching and research capabilities. As a result, other faculty discouraged students from registering for her classes. When one male student started defending the newcomer, male faculty gossiped that his concerns constituted evidence that the newcomer maintained an inappropriate sexual relationship with a student. With reticence, the newcomer filed complaints with the dean concerning harassment and the hostile work environment. Unfortunately, rather than taking the newcomer's side and helping to resolve the problem, the dean redefined the complaint as further indication of the newcomer's inability to fit in with the university. Eventually the newcomer resigned her position and sought work elsewhere.

It is difficult to produce reliable estimates of intentional discrimination and how frequently women are subjected to these types of interactions, but in all likelihood intentional discrimination is underreported. One reason for this underreporting is due to the fact that persons being discriminated against often do not know that they are being harmed, as is usually the case in covert discrimination. Another concern is that there can be retribution for reporting harassment, and therefore many victims suffer quietly.

As important as intentional forms of discrimination are, an overemphasis on this one cause of inequality would lead to limited understanding of the causes of gender inequality and limit the types of social programs to remedy social problems. One concern, for instance, is that focusing only on intentional discrimination implies that institutions are, by and large, operating in a fair and equitable manner toward women and that gender inequality is attributable to the actions of a relatively small number of abusive men. Intentional discrimination is only a partial factor in the overall equation of the causes of gender inequality. Discrimination can also occur even when people mean no ill will to others. In these circumstances, entirely different social responses are implied.

Unintentional Discrimination

Although some people deliberately strive to discriminate against other people, there is considerable evidence that inequality is also due to unintentional actions as well. According to Valian (1998), people commonly interact on the basis of **gender schemas,** unarticulated beliefs. These schemas orient interpretations of men's and women's actions, framing perceptions of individuals in accordance with stereotyped beliefs about men and women. Gender schemas and stereotypes are important to consider because they are instrumental in producing **unintentional discrimination.** By unintentional discrimination, I refer to behaviors that deny fair and equitable treatment, emanating from dispositions that are not necessarily accompanied by ill will or malice on the part of the oppressor.

To illustrate the power of gender schemas, consider the findings of one experiment that involved showing college students a picture of an identically tall man and woman standing next to each other. After viewing the picture, the students were asked to identify which individual was taller. They consistently rated the woman as being shorter than the man (Valian 1998; 2). These students made an inaccurate observation because of their reliance on a gender schema that asserts that women are shorter than men. The students did not know they were making a mistake in their evaluation of the woman, but they made it nonetheless. Similarly, studies reveal that female professors tend to be evaluated less favorably in comparison to male professors on student evaluations (Sidanius and Crane 1989). This finding is especially interesting considering the fact that female professors tend to spend more time and energy on teaching in comparison to their male counterparts (Valian 1998). Why do students rate female professors more critically than they rate male professors? In part, it might be due to biases that incline students to perceive women as less scholarly than the archetype of the (male) professor.

College faculty and administrators are not immune to the influences of gender schemas in making decisions regarding promotion, evaluating research grant applications, and deciding on the tenure of women faculty (Valian 1998). A study in the journal *Nature* revealed that male applicants who applied for a prestigious postdoctoral fellowship were four times more likely to receive the fellowship than female applicants (Wenneras and Wold 1997). The (mostly male) committee awarding the fellowships rated female applicants substantially lower than male applicants. However, when the researchers reanalyzed the applications, taking into account how many publications each applicant had and the prestige of the journals in which these publications were placed, they found something curious. Women should have scored much higher than the evaluations the committee produced. In reality, the average woman would have needed to be 2.5 times more productive than the average male candidate to receive the same competency score attributed by the committee.

Unfortunately, information on what happened in the committee meetings is not available. It is possible that some of the committee members had ill will toward the women candidates and deliberately favored male candidates. A more plausible explanation could be that members of the committee viewed applications on the basis of gender schemas, perceiving women applicants as less competitive compared with male candidates. When the committee members were deciding to select candidates, they were likely doing the same thing that students did when evaluating the heights of the woman and man— they engaged in **statistical discrimination,** making predictions of productivity of individuals based upon their knowledge of the social group's characteristics. This is akin to a taxi driver's refusing to pick up an African American passenger on the basis that African Americans are more likely to have criminal records. The cab driver does not know about the person hailing the cab, but he does know about the group to which the potential passenger belongs. As mentioned earlier, women tend to be less productive than men as indicated by frequency of publication. Women are also more likely to interrupt their careers for raising children, in comparison to men. Knowing this, members of the committee likely viewed each individual woman's candidacy differently than men's, believing in advance that each individual female applicant would be less productive than the male applicants upon receiving the fellowship.

Individual circumstances of unintentional discrimination often appear fairly innocuous, and seem to have only modest effects as isolated events. The real power of unintentional discrimination stems from its pervasiveness and the frequency of its occurrence. Also, acts of unintentional discrimination are connected in meaningful ways and have considerable cumulative effects. According to Valian (1998) very small differences in treatment of female college faculty can accumulate and, in the end, result in large disparities in salary, promotion, and prestige over the long term. If, for instance, after being denied a research fellowship, a woman might be forced to accept a job at a teaching college rather than at the university level. At a teaching college she will likely be required to teach one or two more courses per semester than she would have at the university level. This difference in work expectations, over the long term, will have a profound impact on how many articles she publishes. Couple this with the tendency of her students to evaluate her critically, and her chances of promotion become even more daunting in comparison to an equally qualified male counterpart.

Intentional and unintentional discrimination receive the greatest amount of attention in the media. It is not unusual for shows such as *20/20* or *Prime-Time Live* to feature stories showing equally qualified male and female applicants being treated very differently in job interviews and financial transactions. Even if intentional and unintentional discrimination were elimanated, gender inequality would likely still remain. This would happen because the very rules of conduct expected in organizations, while appearing fair on the surface, undermine women's abilities to match men economically.

Institutional Discrimination

Institutional discrimination occurs through the familiar operations of society, and it is embedded in the rules and norms that guide organizations (Feagin and Feagin 1978). In order to find institutional discrimination, sociological inquiry must critically examine the ways in which institutions normally operate and the practices that insure that men will be evaluated more favorably than women. The most daunting challenge to countering institutional discrimination is that people commonly perceive the customs and rules surrounding employment, pay, and promotion as being equally fair to men and women. Feminist scholars question the accuracy of this assumption.

In order to identify institutionalized forms of discrimination, some feminist theorists suggest that the comparable worth of occupations be examined (England 1985). **Comparable worth** is a way of conceptualizing how much an occupation should ideally pay by comparing that job to other occupations with similar demands. From this perspective, highly demanding jobs that involve skill, danger, or supervision of others should be compensated more highly in comparison to jobs with lower demands. Even if one job is very different from another job in terms of what is actually being done, if it requires similar amounts of education, skill, supervision, etc., both jobs should be compensated at a comparable level. This is not always the case, however. According to England (1985), the sex composition of jobs plays a great influence on the wage levels. The types of jobs that women tend to occupy consistently pay lower wages than the types of jobs men tend to occupy. Sometimes these differences are startling. For example, the job of a registered nurse is more demanding, requires a greater amount of education, is more stressful, and requires greater accountability than the job of an auto mechanic. However, auto mechanics often make more than registered nurses (Aman and England 1997). In California, school librarians (a job that may require a master's degree) sometimes earn less than custodians and groundskeepers (Aman and England 1997). From a feminist perspective, it seems likely that these jobs pay less because they are associated with women's work, which tends to be culturally devalued.

College society provides an excellent laboratory to test the theory of female job devaluation because it allows the application of the comparable worth approach to studying faculty pay. Faculty specialize in a number of different disciplines, but they perform very similar tasks, such as teaching, research, publishing, evaluating students, and serving on committees. Using the comparable worth approach, and if employees are compensated in accordance with the demands of the job, faculty in different departments should earn roughly equal wages. However, if the female devaluation theory is correct, the disciplines where women are concentrated will likely have lower salaries in comparison to disciplines where men are concentrated. Figure 3.4 offers compelling support for the female devaluation theory. Women faculty are most heavily concentrated in education, humanities, and fine arts departments. Faculty in these departments earn considerably less than faculty in the departments with greater concentrations of men. This devaluing of feminized disciplines is one means by which colleges institutionally discriminate against women.

Another way in which institutionalized discrimination occurs on campus concerns the methods administrators use to evaluate faculty. As mentioned above, faculty are expected to engage in a wide variety of activities, and they have considerable discretion concerning which activities to concentrate their efforts on. Women tend to be more involved in teaching and advising, men tend to involve themselves more heavily in research and publication (Valian 1998). University culture, however, tends to devalue teaching in comparison to research. For example, faculty speak of teaching

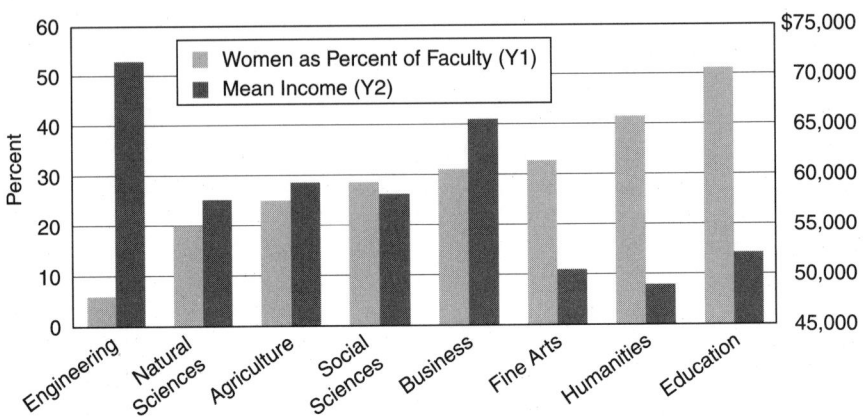

FIGURE 3.4   Academic Disciplines: Mean Income and Percent Female Faculty 1992

Source: U.S. Dept. of Education 1996

"loads" (burdens) as opposed to research "opportunities." These values carry over to administrative decisions concerning faculty compensation and promotion. According to one survey of 245 college and university administrators, student evaluations play an important role in reappointment decisions. However, book and journal article publications play a stronger role in decisions for tenure, promotion, and merit pay (Marchant and Newman 1994). Why is teaching accorded a lower value than research? Drawing upon feminist theory, it may be because teaching is associated with nurturing, a traditional female responsibility.

The devaluing of teaching can also be seen be comparing different types of colleges. Doctoral universities (research Institutions) pay much higher salaries than baccalaureate colleges and two-year college (teaching institutions). For example, in 1999/2000, the average full professor at a doctoral-level university earned $87,022. In comparision, a full professor at a baccalaureate institution earned, on average, $61,775, and a full professor at a two-year college earned only $56,778 (Academe 2000). Not incidentally, women only make up 30% of the faculty at doctoral universities, and tend to be more heavily concentrated in baccalaureate institutions (38%) and two-year colleges (47%) (Academe 2000). There are a variety of factors that influence the higher preponderance of women in teaching colleges, but the institutionalized practice of offering different levels of compensation between these institutions has a profound effect on the overall average earnings of women faculty. In fact, this type of "occupation-establishment" gender segregation is a major cause of the pay gap between women and men in the wider economy (Peterson and Morgan 1995).

Institutionalized discrimination can also occur in the timing of tenure decisions. Tenure grants faculty permanent membership on a college faculty. The decision to grant tenure is typically determined within the first seven years of a faculty member's employment on campus. This is a stressful period, during which junior faculty try to demonstrate their highest potentials in teaching and research. For many faculty women, the pursuit of tenure occurs during the same period in the life course when they are also considering having children. Thus, these coinciding events create greater difficulties for women to advance into these coveted positions (Colander and Woos 1997; Williams 2000). Data support this conclusion. In 1999, women comprised only one in three (35%) associate professors and only one in five (19%) full professors working in American colleges and universities (Academe 2000).

The effects of institutional discrimination are in some ways more profound and daunting than intentional or unintentional discrimination. Unlike the other two forms of discrimination, the concern is not in identifying individuals or small groups who seek to do harm to women. It is embedded in the normal operations of society, practices that tend to devalue women's work and ignore the constraints reproduction and child care responsibilities place upon women. Because institutionalized practices are generally accepted as "normal," they are much harder to remedy in comparison to responding to abusive or prejudiced individuals.

Can Discrimination Be Countered?

There are no simple solutions to complex social problems, and I would caution readers to be skeptical of anyone offering a quick fix. Solutions to problems such as this will necessarily be many faceted and each solution will certainly introduce new concerns. Identifying some sources of the discrimination, however, offers some direction in pursuing its amelioration and remedying a social injustice. In this light, the discussion in this chapter can serve as a catalyst to stir the mind and stimulate further reflection on possibilities for reform.

The recent spate of sexual harassment lawsuits indicates that adults may need formal education about discrimination. Sex discrimination costs employers in a number of ways. One cost stems from litigation and punitive damages that result when abuses occur. Discrimination lawsuits are increasing in frequency and costs are mounting for employers, sometimes resulting in multi-million-dollar settlements. Other costs of sexual discrimination are more hidden. A workplace that has a reputation that it is unfriendly to women will likely have a chilling effect on attracting qualified women as employees. Furthermore, employees who experience discrimination and harassment are more likely to experience psychological and physiological symptoms that can undermine productivity (Gerdes 1995; Landrine and Klonoff 1997). As a consequence of these concerns, employers are increasingly offering programs designed to sensitize employees to the problems of intentional and unintentional discrimination.

Responding to institutionalized discrimination is fraught with many more problems. Recall that institutionalized discrimination is embedded in the ways in which organizations customarily operate. Remedies to institutional discrimination necessarily involve changing taken-for-granted ways of doing things and challenging social customs. The negative response in some quarters to affirmative action programs, for instance, helps illuminate this dilemma.

Affirmative action programs were introduced as a means of overcoming institutionalized discrimination, but these remain unpopular to most Americans (Thernstrom and Thernstrom 1997). Part of the unpopularity stems from a misconception of what affirmative action involves. It is sometimes inaccurately described as a "quota system," with an errant belief that organizations must set aside a specific number of positions for women and minorities, and accept these candidates even if they are unqualified for the position. The program, if conducted as intended, does not do this. It only specifies that minority status is to be used as a "plus" on an applicant's file. If there are two qualified persons for a position, affirmative action programs specify that the organization should favor the minority candidate (Bowen and Bok 1998).

Affirmative action programs may be an effective means of enabling minorities to enter positions where they are underrepresented. One study also indicated that increasing the number of women in administrative positions has a positive impact on leveling of gender inequalities in their colleges as a whole (Kulis 1997). However, affirmative action comes with costs as well. Because Americans believe that their society operates as a meritocracy, affirmative action rubs many people as a policy of favoritism of minorities and women (Thernstrom and Thernstrom 1997). As a consequence it can cast an air of suspicion on female and ethnic minorities who would have achieved their positions of power even without affirmative action programs (Steele 1990).

When women enter male-dominated organizations, there remains a number of institutionalized practices that bias evaluations against them. As discussed above, women are much more likely to experience role conflicts as they try to straddle the world of work and the traditionally feminine tasks of housekeeping and childcare. The trick for organizations involves restructuring evaluation procedures in such a way that women are not unfairly penalized for engaging in socially vital activities involved in childcare. An obvious, but highly problematic, solution is to use different sets of standards when evaluating men and women. For example, in the State University of New York system, women, minorities, and Vietnam-era veterans can apply for a one-semester paid leave of absence in order to prepare their tenure portfolios. This paid leave of absence in effect gives these faculty a full semester free of all other responsibilities, such as teaching classes, advising, and committee work. The same opportunity is not extended to younger white males. As a consequence, this program can be construed as discriminatory against non-minorities who could be equally disadvantaged. A single white male raising a child, for instance, would not be eligible for this sabbatical.

Colander and Woos (1997) offer some alternatives to this approach that may be worth considering. For example, organizations could potentially establish positions with sensitivity to the demands that confront parents engaged in childcare (see also Bailyn 1997). For instance, rather than restricting tenure-track jobs to full-time positions, colleges could partition a share of these jobs to be half-time positions. The positions would be attractive to many employees (of either sex) who have child-care responsibilities. Accomplishments and compensation could be evaluated in accordance with the expectations of that position. Time-shared jobs, which involve two or more employees working part-time, could also potentially prove effective at helping parents balance the competing demands of family and work. Daycare at the workplace can also help alleviate some problems. Again, these types of remedies are not without concerns. In an era of cost cutting both in private industry and in academia, administrators continue to concentrate on minimizing expenses. Time-share jobs and daycare may increase the costs of running the organization.

Institutionalized discrimination also operates by devaluing the worth of women's work. This may prove even more difficult to remedy. As discussed above, female faculty earn less, in part, because they are concentrated in positions that are undervalued. They also earn less because they are more likely to concentrate on undervalued activities such as teaching as opposed to research. One approach for making immediate remedies could involve distributing across-the-board salary increases to all female faculty working at the institution until the pay gap is eliminated (Feree and McQuillan 1998). However, as with other quick fixes, this solution is likely to be met with a strong reaction by other employees who do not receive the salary increase.

A different approach could involve an assessment of the comparable worth of jobs. If two different types of jobs require similar amounts of education, responsibility, skill, etc., some analysts believe they should be compensated accordingly (Aman and England 1998). The assessments would be made in consideration of gender compositions of jobs, identifying those job categories in which women are concentrated. These occupations could then be examined to determine if there is a considerable pay disparity with comparable male-dominated jobs. According to this model, pay is adjusted not by virtue of one's status as a man or woman, but rather in accordance with the responsibilities of the job. Under this approach, a man working in an undervalued female profession would likely receive an increase in compensation along with the other women working in that job category. A woman working in a male-dominated profession would be less likely to receive an increase in compensation.

As theoretical abstractions, these approaches seem plausible. Their application in the "real" world, however, may be more difficult to put into effect. For instance, I have suggested that professors all perform remarkably similar work, yet male-dominated disciplines tend to pay more than female- dominated disciplines. The comparable worth approach suggests that the salaries in the humanities and education departments should be raised to match the salaries offered in computer science and engineering departments. Unfortunately, colleges and universities do not have unlimited resources. To make adjustments of this magnitude could bankrupt a budget. Colleges also have real world concerns of attracting employees who could potentially make considerably more money in the private sector. A college seeking to establish a computer science or engineering department will be hard-pressed to attract suitable faculty if compensation is comparable with that typically offered within education or communications departments.

Gender inequality is not an intractable problem, but it is certainly a challenging issue to address. Solutions to the problem require recognizing that the differences between men and women are largely socially constructed. It is also important to establish clear policies for dealing with unfair treatment of women. Perhaps the most challenging direction for change involves identifying and rectifying institutionalized forms of discrimination. So long as "feminine" work is undervalued, women will continue to earn less than men in academia and in the wider economy.

REFERENCES

AAUW. 1992. *How Schools Shortchange Girls: The AAUW Report.* New York: Marlowe and Company.

Academe 2000. "More Good News, So Why the Blues?: The Annual Report on the Economic Status of the Profession 1999–2000." *Academe.* 86:12–95.

Aman, Carolyn and Paula England. 1997. "Comparable Worth: When Do Two Jobs Deserve the Same Pay?" in Benokraitis, Nijole [ed.] *Subtle Sexism: Current Practice and Prospects for Change.* Thousand Oaks: Sage.

Bailyn, Lotte. 1997. "The Impact of Corporate Culture on Work-Family Integration" in Parasuraman J. H. Saroj *Integrating Work and Family.* Westport, Connecticut: Quorum Books.

Beall, Anne. 1993. "The Social Construction of Gender" in Beall, Anne and Ellen Berscheid [ed.] *The Psychology of Gender.* New York: Guilford Press.

Benokraitis, Nijole. 1997. "Sex Discrimination in the 21st Century" in Benokraitis, Nijole [ed.], *Subtle Sexism: Current Practice and Prospects for Change.* Thousand Oaks: Sage.

Bowen, William and Derek Bok. 1998. *The Shape of the River: Long-Term Consequences of Considering Race in College and University Admissions.* Princeton, N.J.: Princeton University Press.

Cahill, Spencer. 1987. "Children and Civility: Ceremonial Deviance and the Acquisition of Ritual Competence." *Social Psychological Quarterly.* 50:312–321.

Charon, Joel. 1995. *Symbolic Interactionism: An Introduction, An Interpretation, An Integration.* Englewood Cliffs, NJ: Prentice Hall.

Chodorow, Nancy. 1978. *The Reproduction of Mothering.* Berkeley: University of California Press.

Colander, David and Joanna Wayland Woos. 1997. "Institutional Demand-Side Discrimination against Women and the Human Capital Model." *Feminist Economics.* 3:53–64.

Coontz, Stephanie. 1992. *The Way We Never Were: American Families and the Nostalgia Trap.* New York: Basic Books.

DeKeseredy, Walter. 1990. "Male Peer Support and Woman Abuse: The Current State of Knowledge." *Sociological Focus.* 23:129–139.

England, Paula. 1985. "The Sex Gap in Work and Wages." *Society.* 22:68–74.

Feagin, Joe and Clairece Booher Feagin. 1978. *Discrimination American Style: Institutional Racism and Sexism.* Englewood Cliffs: Prentice Hall.

Ferree, Myra Marx and Julia McQuillan. 1998. "Gender-Based Pay Gaps: Methodological and Policy Issues in University Salary Studies." *Gender and Society.* 12:7–39.

Fiorentine, Robert and Stephen Cole. 1992. "Why Fewer Women Become Physicians: Explaining the Premed Persistence Gap." *Sociological Forum.* 7:469–496.

Gallant, Mary and Jay Cross. 1993. "Wayward Puritans in the Ivory Tower: Collective Aspects of Gender Discrimination in Academia." *Sociological Quarterly.* 34:237–256.

Gerdes, Eugenia Proctor. 1995. "Women Preparing for Traditionally Male Professions: Physical and Psychological Symptoms Associated with Work and Home." *Sex Roles.* 32:787–807.

Giroux, Henry. 1997. "Are Disney Movies Good for Your Kids?" in Steinberg, Shirley and Joe Kincheloe [ed.] *Kinderculture: The Corporate Construction of Childhood.* Boulder, CO: Westview Press.

Hochschild, Arlie with Anne Machung. 1989. *The Second Shift: Working Parents and the Revolution at Home.* New York: Viking.

Kanter, Rosabeth Moss. 1977. *Men and Women of the Corporation.* New York: Basic Books.

Kulis, Stephen. 1997. "Gender Segregation Among College and University Employees." *Sociology of Education.* 70:151–173.

Landrine, Hope and Elizabeth Klonoff. 1997. *Discrimination Against Women: Prevalence, Consequences and Remedies.* Thousand Oaks: Sage.

Lorber, Judith. 1994. Paradoxes of Gender. New Haven: Yale University Press.

Lott, Bernice and Diane Maluso. 1993. "The Social Learning of Gender" in Beall, Anne and Ellen Berscheid [ed.], *The Psychology of Gender.* New York: Guilford Press.

Marchant, Gregory and Isadore Newman. 1994. "Faculty Activities and Rewards: Views from Education Administrators in the USA." *Assessment and Evaluation in Higher Education.* 19:140–152.

Moen, Phyllis and Penny Becker. 1999. "Scaling Back: Dual-Earner Couples' Work-Family Strategies." *Journal of Marriage and the Family.* 61:995–1007.

National Center for Education Statistics. 1996. *Education Statistics on Disk; 1996 Edition.* Washington, DC: U.S. Department of Education.

National Science Foundation. 1999. *Women, Minorities, and Persons with Disabilities in Science and Engineering: 1988.* Arlington, VA: NSF 99-338.

Peterson, Trond and Laurie Morgan. 1995. "Separate and Unequal: Occupation-Establishment Sex Segregation and the Gender Wage Gap." *American Journal of Sociology.* 101:329–365.

Orenstein, Peggy. 1994. *School Girls: Young Women, Self-Esteem, and the Confidence Gap.* New York: Anchor Books.

Reskin, Barbara and Irene Padavic. 1994. *Women and Men at Work.* Thousand Oaks: Pine Forge Press .

Rhode, Deborah. 1997. *Speaking of Sex: The Denial of Gender Inequality.* Cambridge, MA: Harvard University Press.

Schor, Juliet. 1991. *The Overworked American: The Unexpected Decline of Leisure.* New York: Basic Books.

Sidanius, J. and M. Crane. 1989. "Job Evaluation and Gender: The Case of University Faculty." *Journal of Applied Social Psychology* 19:174–197.

Stack, Carol. 1997. *All Our Kin.* New York: Basic Books.

Steele, Shelby. 1990. *The Content of Our Character: A New Vision of Race in America.* New York: HarperCollins.

Thernstrom, Stephan and Abigail Thernstrom. 1997. *America in Black and White: One Nation, Indivisible.* New York: Simon & Schuster.

U.S. Department of Education. 1995. "Faculty Salaries, Tenure and Fringe Benefits of Full Time Instructional Faculty." An Integrated Postsecondary Education Data System.

U.S. Bureau of Census. 1998. Statistical Abstract of the United States: 1998. Washington DC.

Valian, Virginia. 1998. *Why So Slow?: The Advancement of Women.* Cambridge, MA: MIT Press.

Wenneras, Christine and Agnes Wold. 1997. "Nepotism and Sexism in Peer-Review." *Nature.* 387:341–343.

Williams, Joan. 2000. *Unbending Gender: Why Family and Work Conflict and What To Do About It.* New York: Oxford U. Press.

4 The Janus Face of College Bureaucracy

For the senior who is headed for the corporation it is almost as if it were part of one master scheme. The locale shifts; the training continues, for at the same time that the colleges have been changing their curriculum to suit the corporation, the corporation has responded by setting up its own campuses and classrooms. By now the two have been so well molded that it's difficult to tell where one leaves off and the other begins.

—William H. Whyte, *The Organization Man* (1956; p. 63)

Colleges and universities are, at times, crazily bureaucratic. This fact is apparent to many students who have attempted to drop or add a course after a deadline, who have tried to protest a grade received, who have attempted to switch majors, or who have tried to get credits transferred from one institution to another. In many circumstances, these activities flow with surprising speed and precision. In other circumstances (which tend to be more memorable) the process gets bogged down in paperwork, or entails shuttling complaints from one office to another until a receptive administrator finally expedites the necessary processes.

Colleges are especially interesting to study because they are partially responsible for molding what William H. Whyte termed "the organization man," the type of person who fits into the bureaucratic order of modern society like a cog in a great machine. One wonders why colleges operate in this fashion, why the bureaucratic operations seem so cumbersome, and why the bureaucrats seem so heartless. Certainly there must be a reason that our society has developed into this web of interconnected bureaucracies, linking together health systems, schools, governments, police departments, courts, the military, and business. Literally, from cradle to grave, our lives intersect with bureaucracies. What implication does this have for us and for the well-being of society?

Seldom are bureaucratic operations fun, but, in the end, they usually work to a greater or lesser degree. Transcripts are sent, meal plans are accounted, and roommates are assigned. Less visible to students, but the bane of many a faculty member and administrator, are the piles of paperwork and committee assignments that tie up the hours and distract them from the activities they like best, teaching and research. It is little wonder that the term bureaucracy implies wastefulness, slow process, red tape, and a bundle of other frustrating experiences endemic to living in the modern world.

College society lays bare the paradoxical nature of bureaucracies, processes that simultaneously liberate and constrain members of society. It reveals the contrasting social impacts of bureaucratization, a situation that calls to mind the ancient Roman god Janus. Janus, you may recall, is that odd-looking fellow with two faces, one looking forward and the other looking backward. As Janus faces backward, he assesses where we were, looking back through the doorway of time. As Janus looks forward, he sees the future and where we are going. In the case of bureaucracy, Janus' assessment of bureaucracy would no doubt be complex, as he would simultaneously observe rational organizations that generate high levels of productivity, as well as the irrationality of dehumanized relationships. This chapter places bureaucratic operations in a historical context, examining the origins of bureaucratic rationality, its effects on present-day life, and the directions it may lead society.

A Historical Look Back: College Life Prior to Bureaucratization

Before discussing and defining bureaucracy, maybe it would be helpful to step back a couple hundred years to see what college life was like in the relative absence of bureaucracy. Looking at the early years of Harvard, the oldest college in American society, offers some glimpses of organizational conduct in a comparatively nonbureaucratic university. What occurred at Harvard in the seventeenth, eighteenth, and nineteenth centuries exemplifies changes that occurred in other colleges and organizations throughout American society.

Harvard started as a small college in the 1600s, and through the early 1800s it differed from the modern university in a number of respects. The early Harvard existed in an era when instructional and research technology were rudimentary, and the collective pool of knowledge was quite limited. As an indication of this, consider that, in 1723, Harvard's first library card catalogue was simply a list of titles arranged by size alphabetically in Latin. It wasn't until much later that the university developed a system of classifying books according to subject matter (Battles 2000). Because the collective pool of knowledge was so limited, it was not necessary for students to be taught by professors who specialized in a discipline. Instead, they were instructed by tutors who had read and demonstrated mastery of a limited set of texts from different disciplines (Bailyn 1986). Unlike a modern university, there were no departments, such as an astronomy department or biology department; there were simply tutors and students.

Whereas present-day Harvard is designed to produce captains of industry, science, and politics, early Harvard was charged with socializing boys into respectable young men (Handlin 1986). To serve this end, tutors organized their classes as recitations, and discipline was accorded more importance than transmitting cutting-edge knowledge. Classes involved little more than students reiterating memorized passages of preselected texts, often the same texts that the tutors themselves had memorized when they were students. As a consequence it was not a particularly stimulating intellectual environment for students or faculty.

Early Harvard was a much smaller institution than today's large complex university. In 1718 Harvard only enrolled a total of 124 students and by 1810, the graduating class still numbered only 63 students (Morrison 1936). Its wealth was also limited, and its endowment did not grow significantly until the mid-nineteenth century (Thernstrom 1986). Harvard also had presidents who felt free (and perhaps obligated) to intrude into even the most minute aspects of its operations. Early presidents, for example, often taught classes and knew individual students intimately. One has to wonder how many present-day college presidents know many of their college's students by name, let alone know what goes on in the classrooms of their institutions.

Today, one of Harvard's most valuable possessions is its name. Surprisingly, for nearly a century, Harvard did not establish a clear identity, and it was called a variety of names, including "Harvard College," "The College in Cambridge," or simply the "College or Academy." Sometimes even individual halls were deemed different "colleges" (Bailyn 1986). Imagine McDonald's being unsure of what to call itself or changing its corporate name with little deliberation!

Like their present-day counterparts, many of the early Harvard students seemed more interested in drinking than in their classes, and citizens of Boston complained about their unruly behavior. Like students of today, early Harvard students also complained about their food. What did differ, though, was the way students expressed their complaints. Whereas students of today might send around a petition or complain about their food to a Dean of Student Life, in 1818 Harvard students rioted and broke nearly all of the college's crockery (Bailyn 1986). Harvard students also had to deal with poor teachers and boring classes, something that is probably familiar to many modern students as well. But unlike their modern counterparts, early Harvard students did not have access to teaching evaluations and were not likely to lodge formal complaints. The students responded in what would seem today to be a peculiar path of action—they formed their own learning clubs! Instead of relying on their tutors, students met in groups in each other's rooms to discuss new ideas, write poetry, collect libraries, compose music, and do a variety of other physical and intellectual activities.

How did Harvard survive those early years without bureaucracy? In part, it had to do with being comparably small, and the nature of its endeavor, which required only modest amounts of money, modest technological expertise, and little codependency between employees. This is not to imply that Harvard was unorganized, however. Organization did exist, but in a very different form than the complex bureaucratic system present today. Unlike the modern Harvard, it maintained order through a combination of coercion, tradition, and charismatic leadership.

According to Weber, there are essentially two general ways to get a person to do something they might otherwise avoid doing, through coercion or through authority (Gerth and Mills 1946). **Coercion** involves the use of force to gain obedience. For example, a robber can coerce a person to surrender his or her money with the threat of violence. Likewise, early administrators at Harvard were not opposed to using coercive techniques to control their students. For instance, four disobedient students who were found responsible for the food riot of 1818 were flogged. In 1823, after experiencing many problems with students, the president of Harvard expelled half of the senior class. In other circumstances, parents were fined if their child was not suitably prepared for class. Obviously Harvard students were interested in avoiding punishment and therefore tended to be compliant to basic expectations, such as attending recitations. Coercion did not stop students from drinking and frequenting prostitutes, however, largely because college officials had difficulty policing students off campus (Handlin 1986).

On the surface, coercion seems an effective strategy of controlling students (do this or else!), but in practice coercion is a very limited means of producing compliance. Michel Foucault (1977) points out that social order based on coercion has an underlying contradiction that undermines control. The greater the frequency that coercive techniques of control are used, the more hostility is built up between the controller and the controlled. Thinking of social control at Harvard in this way reveals a huge cost of coercing students. Harvard in 1800 only had $250,000 in assets (Thernstrom 1986). As any college fund-raiser knows, a large proportion of the assets of a college or university come through alumni donations. If the college is a coercive institution, frequently fining and flogging students, it would greatly reduce the likelihood that students would later give donations to their alma mater. In order for Harvard to be a successful college, it needed to build loyalty, not hostility, among its graduates. This is one reason why Harvard today spends literally millions of dollars each year on class reunions (Trumpbour 1989).

Weber suggested that people could be ruled in ways that would not necessarily make them angry or discontented. To build a healthy institution requires the wholehearted commitment of members of that organization. This involves forming power relationships based upon authority rather than coercion. **Authority** is more effective in producing social control because it establishes the legitimacy of the persons in power. If people believe that an individual or group of individuals has a justifiable right to tell them how to behave, they will conform and will also harbor no ill will toward those in the commanding positions. Weber suggested that there are three overarching authority systems. Two of these systems are ancient, traditional authority and charismatic authority, and one system is thoroughly modern, legal-rational authority (Gerth and Mills 1946). Harvard in the early years relied much more heavily on traditional authority and charismatic authority than on legal-rational authority.

Traditional authority is based upon time-honored practices passed from one generation to the next. Under this system, the ruler's power to lead and direct others is vested in social customs asserting his or her right to rule. In premodern Europe and Africa, for instance, a king's leadership is transmitted in a progenitor system whereby power passed from father to son. Even today in England and Japan, although the roles are now reduced to largely ceremonial functions, kingships and emperorships continue to be passed down along family lines.

Harvard was not ruled in the early years solely by traditional authority, but an early president of Harvard offers an interesting example of how traditional authority can be exercised. Increase Mather, president of Harvard in 1692, sought to increase his social status, as well as that of the college. Using his position as president strategically, he wrote a charter that stipulated that the Harvard Corporation could "grant and admit Academical Degrees, as in the Universities in England" (Bailyn 1986; 11). Immediately following this declaration, Mather ordered the Harvard Corporation to confer upon him a doctoral degree because he owned many books and "because he had rendered himself for his Learning and Merits, the object of highest commendation, not only among the American, but among the European Churches" (Bailyn 1986; 11). This strikes modern sensitivities as a blatant abuse of power, as Mather essentially conferred upon himself his own degree. Under traditional authority, however, there is little to bar a president from granting himself a doctorate because there were few rules existing that would prevent such an obvious self-serving action. Because tradition largely established that a leader of a university would be able to do what he feels is best, Mather let tradition work as the basis of his decision to advance himself through decree.

Charismatic authority is another means of controlling people. According to Weber, this system of control operates through a leader who is believed to have extraordinary or supernatural powers. Such an individual is considered to have exceptional insight into the workings of people and society. Classic examples of charismatic leaders include Jesus, Mahatma Gandhi, and Martin Luther King, Jr. Charismatic authority does not rely on technical qualifications for the job, such as having a degree or relevant job experience, nor is it based on tradition. Few Indians, for instance, asked Mahatma Gandhi for his resumé or were concerned about his family lineage before choosing to follow him. A modern university president, however, will need to substantiate his or her qualifications before entering the position of power.

In the early days at Harvard, selection of presidents was considerably influenced by their charismatic power. The historian Bernard Bailyn describes an early Harvard president in this way:

> James Thorton Kirkland (A.B. 1789, President 1810–1828), a Unitarian minister, was the most popular, the most beloved president Harvard has ever had. He was a man of extraordinary charm, an easy and witty conversationalist, sensible, humane, tolerant, endlessly cheerful, open to change, devoted to his responsibilities and to the college in all its aspects.

Upon Kirkland's resignation from Harvard, following an unsuccessful and tumultuous battle against the Harvard Corporation, members of the senior class penned a touching testimonial, reading in part:

> We thank you sir, imperfectly, but heartily. We thank you for the honors which your award has made more sweet, and we thank you for the reproof which has been tempered with love. We thank you for the benignity of manners which engaged our confidence, for the charities which secured our hearts. We thank you, sir, for all the little, nameless, unremembered acts of your kindness and authority. We are deeply in your debt, but the obligation is not irksome; it is a debt of gratitude we are well pleased to owe. (Bailyn 1986; 43)

Kirkland was lauded for his personal qualities in both accounts. He was the kind of person people liked having in a position of power, but not much is said of his skills as an administrator. Nor is much mention made of any specific accomplishments. What is emphasized is his intimate contact with students, who knew him on a personal level and liked him. In reality, his success as president was more closely tied to his charismatic power than to his ability to chart a path for Harvard's future (Bailyn 1986).

Certainly Kirkland did accomplish some important things. Prior to his administration, the Harvard commons was known for its outhouses, pigs, and litter, and by the end of his administration Harvard had an attractive campus. However, in the early 1800s, Harvard experienced increasing faculty dissent over issues of job security and professional autonomy. It was also a period of student protest over recitation-based classes, which they deemed an outmoded institutional practice. There was also considerable mismanagement of Harvard's investments under Kirkland's administration and this proved very costly to the institution. Ultimately these and other problems prompted the Board of Overseers to investigate his administration. After a bitter confrontation, during which one of the investigators supposedly called the president an imbecile, Kirkland resigned.

Kirkland failed Harvard because he did not formulate a framework to bring Harvard into correspondence with the needs of an industrializing nation (Bailyn 1986). In the emerging society, boys did not just want to be made into cultured men, they also wanted to be made into professionals. Not only was Harvard relying on outmoded methods of instruction, it was also losing distinguished faculty to competing institutions. If Kirkland were a modern-day president, it is extremely unlikely that he would have been able to hold on to his position of authority for as long as he did. Looking back to an earlier time, we see that Kirkland provides a poignant illustration of the declining relevance of charismatic authority as a means of guiding an organization in the modern era.

According to Weber, modern society is increasingly organized around legal-rational authority. **Legal-rational authority** is based on rules that stipulate that a person, by virtue of holding a particular position in an organization, has the right to exercise power in formally stated ways within that organization. This system relies on rules, usually written down, that direct people to lead and follow. These rules are tied to an overarching rational plan that is put in place for the sake of organizational efficiency.

At the end of Kirkland's term as president, legal-rational authority supplanted tradition and charisma. In 1823, the overseers of Harvard College sought to determine why Kirkland was having so many difficulties leading the institution. They concluded that the president had too much discretion to meddle in all affairs of the college. They also determined that there were not enough rules to guide the workings of the organization. They recommended that the president be relieved of everyday administrative responsibilities and that these responsibilities be given to other members of the administration and faculty. In other words, the president of Harvard was no longer free to micromanage college social relations, or have the liberty to rule any aspect of college life that he saw fit. To be efficient, everyday responsibilities would be divided among different offices and the president would be charged with the "general superintendence" and general policy matters (Bailyn 1986; 35). In the modern era, the president of Harvard was to have a much more narrowly defined role in university life.

The committee also recommended that the teaching staff be reorganized according to subject matter. Under Kirkland and previous presidents, instructors were an unorganized set of general tutors. The committee recommended that the college be restructured into organizational subunits called departments. Each department was to be headed by a senior professor, who would supervise a number of instructors specializing in that discipline. Furthermore, a rigorous examination system would be instituted to make students accountable for learning subject matter. Vacations would be limited to 10 weeks and acceptable numbers of absences would be specified. In short, the committee suggested that a system of well-thought-out rules to replace an older system that relied too heavily on coercion, tradition, and the charismatic authority of individual presidents. In short, the overseers recommended restructuring Harvard into a modern bureaucracy.

The transformations that occurred at Harvard in the nineteenth century corresponded not only with the types of transformations taking place at other colleges and universities; they also corresponded with revolutionary changes in the organization of businesses in American society. As American society was transforming from its agrarian roots into an industrial superpower, its approach to regulating the workplace shifted in remarkable ways. Without bureaucracy, industries and colleges would remain small, simple, and inefficient. With bureaucracy, systems were created that could regulate large numbers of people and engage them effectively in complex interconnected tasks.

Bureaucracies as Rational Organizations

Early Harvard worked, but it did not work nearly as well as the modern-day institution. In comparison, the modern Harvard is run much more like a major corporation (Weissman 1989), and is organized according to bureaucratic principles. To understand the advantages of this organizational form, it is necessary to examine the principles underpinning bureaucratic organization. Systems of mass production and scientific management, two features of modern industrial America made possible by bureaucracy, offer telling information on the impact of bureaucratic rationality, and its positive and negative consequences.

Bureacracy as an Ideal Type

Max Weber theorized that the prevalence of legal-rational authority in modern society was intricately linked with the rise of bureaucratic organizations (Gerth and Mills 1946). But what exactly is a bureaucracy? Weber answered this question using a tool he termed the ideal type. An **ideal type** is a conceptual description of the central features of a category of things to be studied. This description enables theorists to identify the core aspects of the objects in question. Weber identified his ideal type bureaucracy as having the following important characteristics: efficiency, division of labor, hierarchy of positions, governance by rules, employment based on technical qualifications, and impersonality.

Efficiency. Efficiency is the guiding force behind bureaucratic organization. Bureaucracies are designed to perform complex tasks and are structured to accomplish these tasks in an expeditious and cost-effective manner. Despite their reputation as being inefficient, in most circumstances bureaucracies are actually very good at doing extremely complicated tasks, at least in comparison to more primitive organizational forms. These things are not reflected upon very often, but consider the numerous (and often complicated) tasks expected of colleges and universities. Simply in terms of expediting instruction, this involves employing professors, issuing paychecks, housing and feeding students, assigning classes to rooms, ordering books, assigning roommates, issuing grade reports, filing of transcripts, etc. Given how complex these tasks are, the degree to which colleges and universities accomplish these tasks successfully is remarkable. The goal of efficiency is especially important to identify as a characteristic of the ideal type bureaucracy because it is the overarching explanation for the other aspects of its organizational structure.

Division of Labor. One way in which organizations achieve efficiency is by dividing work among employees. Bureaucracies achieve this by assigning people to positions or offices. Each position is associated with the performance of a very limited set of tasks that the officeholder is expected to perform. At colleges, for instance, professors are charged with tasks relating to the instruction and evaluation of students. The registrar is charged with maintaining academic records, structuring room assignments, and establishing the academic calendar. The bursar keeps track of the financial affairs of the institution. Resident assistants are responsible for sections of halls. Dividing labor enables people to specialize, and through specialization efficiency is created. Kirkland's Harvard had a very low division of labor; modern colleges have a high division of labor.

Hierarchy of Positions. Bureaucracies assign power in a hierarchical fashion. Usually a bureaucracy will produce a formal organizational chart that shows how positions are accountable to other positions. Orders from above are transmitted down through a clearly defined chain of command to the appropriate departments and a clearly defined power structure enables bureaucracies to minimize miscommunication of priorities. This structure offers advantages in that it produces accountability of officeholders. In colleges, students know they are accountable to their professors. Professors know that they are accountable to their department chairs. Chairs are accountable to their deans. Deans are accountable to the provost, and the provost is accountable to the president.

Governance by Rules.   Bureaucratic organizations develop rules, usually codified into a book of policies. These rules establish responsibilities of officeholders and the relationships of one officeholder to another. Unlike the rules that guide traditional authority, these policies are systematically planned to achieve technical efficiency. Colleges regulate students and employees in numerous ways and develop formalized procedures to expedite the solutions to problems. For example, sexual harassment can be a problem for students and most colleges have developed a set of procedures to deal with complaints. The rules are not arbitrarily created; they stem from committee decisions with an eye toward structuring policies that increase the ability of the bureaucracy to shield its members from abuses of power.

Employment Based on Technical Qualifications.   Bureaucracies employ people on the basis of their ability to perform tasks assigned to positions. This has obvious advantages over other systems such as the "spoils system" (employment based on political alliances) or nepotism (employment based on kinship relations) because office holders must document capabilities for dependable job performance. Professors, for example, are usually expected to have a Ph.D. at the time of appointment and to be able to document success in teaching and/or research. Students are expected to provide documentation of graduating from high school, as well as transcripts and SAT scores.

Impersonality.   Bureaucracies are impersonal and they prohibit members from bending the rules to unfairly favor one individual over another. Given the same situation, bureaucracies will respond to any two individuals in the exact same manner. In this way, bureaucracies are structured to be fair institutions, treating all members impartially. A professor, for instance, may like one student more than others. In other circumstances a professor's and student's values may clash. The professor's tendency might be to give the abrasive student a worse grade than the more likeable student, but colleges demand that all students be evaluated impartially according to the same standards.

I suspect that many readers will be recalling ways in which their college has failed to fully correspond with Weber's ideal type bureaucracy. The fact is that all bureaucracies will deviate to a greater or lesser extent from the ideal type Weber described. These deviations, however, are seldom strong enough to challenge the fact that bureaucracies are playing an ever more important role in structuring and organizing social relationships, and that bureaucracies tend to operate in the ways Weber described.

Mass Production and Scientific Management

Accompanying the social transformation to a bureaucratic society was a shift from small-scale production methods to mass-production techniques (Chandler 1990). Manufacturers such as Henry Ford learned that there were economic advantages to producing commodities in large volume, and bureaucratic rationality made these complex activities possible. In order to achieve the highest levels of efficiency, Henry Ford and other industrialists reshaped their organizations from the craft production methods of the nineteenth century. One particularly notable example is the development and application of the assembly line, which enabled the mass production of a variety of products ranging from refrigerators to automobiles (Shaiken 1984).

In the early twentieth century, public schools and colleges started to model themselves after mass-production industries as they looked for ways to systematically process large numbers of students (Marshall and Tucker 1992). One indication of how mass production affected educational practices is reflected in the shift away from small schools to large schools, and how large lecture halls replaced the small classes of the nineteenth century. For instance, Cornell University Professor James Maas currently lectures to nearly 1,500 students in the Bailey Hall Auditorium, making his Introduction to Psychology course the largest live lecture course at any American college. Just like factory systems of mass production, schools process students in large volume in order to make education efficient and cost effective. In the modern school, comparable with the modern factory, students are passed from teacher to teacher and from class to class through the organizational equivalent of a conveyor belt.

Mass production, coupled with **scientific management** (often termed **Taylorization**), offered an innovative new approach to structuring work tasks. First developed in the early twentieth century by Frederic Winslow Taylor, scientific management uses experimentation and measurement as means of finding the most efficient method of production. Taylor's approach was simple and effective. He believed that if managers could observe workers, and manipulate workers' tasks systematically, managers could develop the ideal conditions to maximize production. The manager, for instance, might manipulate the placement of parts for workers to assemble. Armed with a stopwatch, the manager would then determine the effects changing these activities had upon worker productivity. In a number of famous experiments, Taylor was able to demonstrate that scientific management could dramatically increase worker productivity, sometimes by as much as 400% (Taylor 1911/1964).

To make their businesses run as efficiently as possible, Taylor suggested that managers restructure the work so that companies would not need to rely on any individual worker's talents (Taylor 1911/1964). For example, rather than training workers to know how to assemble all of the parts of a car, as would have been the norm under nineteenth-century craft production, Taylor suggested that each worker specialize in a single small task, such as putting on lug nuts. From Taylor's perspective, dissociating the work tasks from the skills of individual workers was advantageous because it enabled managers to gain control over the pace of production. If, for example, a worker chose to work at a leisurely pace, Taylor's new system made it possible for managers to fire that worker and immediately hire someone else to take over the job. Because the new worker would need little training, all workers became replaceable, something not possible when production required the employment of skilled craftsmen. Henry Ford's use of a Taylorized production process, organizing work around simple tasks performed by unskilled workers, enabled him to produce huge profits in an industry plagued with low quality, high costs, and slow output. His Model T was manufactured inexpensively. His workers needed little training, labored at a grueling pace, and accepted wages much lower than those demanded by skilled mechanics. In terms of bureaucratic rationality, this made great sense. A critic of scientific management termed this process as the "deskilling" of work (Braverman 1974), a concern I will return to later.

According to Marshall and Tucker (1992), educational administrators adopted the same principle in designing instructional strategies for primary and secondary school teachers. One means of deskilling teaching involves segregating teachers into discrete subject areas and grade levels. For instance, rather than hiring a teacher with a breadth of knowledge (i.e., a science teacher conversant in chemistry, physics, and biology), schools now seek a narrow type of teacher (i.e., a seventh-grade biology teacher). This new teacher only needs to know a very restricted body of literature to perform his or her job correctly. Colleges operate in a similar manner, and the tendency is to structure positions into restricted specializations. For instance, colleges seek specialists in subdisciplines such as deviance or gender studies, rather than social scientists. Largely gone are the days when a college would seek professors capable of demonstrating a depth of knowledge in the many substantive areas that extend beyond their specialty. Given that the job of teaching seventh-grade biology or a course in juvenile delinquency is similar one year to the next, the job of a teacher and professor becomes somewhat similar to the job of a laborer in Henry Ford's factory.

Taylor also suggested managers adopt a principle of "separating conception from execution." In a scientifically managed work environment, thinking is separated from doing and there is an organizational division between those who think (managers) and those who labor (workers). Schools, in many ways, also separate conception from execution. There is surprisingly little discretion involved in teaching primary and secondary schools because many of the tasks of teaching are prescribed. For instance, in many schools tenth-grade English teachers are expected to teach specific books to their students, not books of their own choosing. Also, substantial portions of curricular materials are designed by textbook companies, reducing teaching to displaying, handing out, and collecting premanufactured materials. The implications are that many teachers exert surprisingly little discretion over what they teach and how they teach it. The same is somewhat true at the college level. Even at the college level, thanks to a competitive textbook market, introductory textbooks offer ready templates for structuring course readings. Included with these texts are test banks, transparencies, power point presentations, videotapes, lesson plans, and a variety of other curricular materials. Given the degree to which college courses are predesigned and supported with ready-made lesson plans and tests, it is entirely possible to teach an introductory course with only a rudimentary understanding of the discipline.

The Irrational Consequences of Bureaucratization

Thus far, I have been deliberately one-sided in my description of bureaucratic rationality, mass production, and scientific management, highlighting the capacity these practices extend to accomplishing complex tasks. I have also suggested that they are much better at accomplishing their goals than were earlier organizational forms. But if bureaucracies are so rational, why do they have such a bad reputation? Finding an answer requires revisiting some classic sociological studies that directly examine the everyday workings of bureaucracies. Case studies of actual bureaucracies reveal a multitude of irrational consequences. To facilitate inquiry, I adopt a critical sociological perspective. **Critical sociology** is an approach to studying society with a keen eye, identifying those aspects of culture and structure that undermine mankind's ability to live to its fullest potential. As a rule, critical sociologists adopt a skeptical position, looking at existing social arrangements as possibly impinging on the potential of individuals to construct positive forms of interaction such as friendship, trust, and cooperation. If bureaucracies are efficient, critical sociology offers a means to examine if this efficiency benefits all social groups equitably.

Dehumanization

Bureaucratic rationality apparently involves a trade-off. Regulation and impersonality promote fairness and efficiency, but at the same time these practices estrange people from one another. As any student who has waited in a registration line knows, much of the interaction in bureaucracies can be characterized as cold and heartless, as opposed to warm and friendly. Ironically, in an effort to liberate mankind through efficiency, bureaucracies dehumanize social relations. An extreme example of this process is offered by Goffman's (1961) accounts of social relations in hospitals. Doctors and nurses, on the whole, are caring people who wish to alleviate patient suffering, and this is why many choose to enter the medical profession (Becker et al. 1961). Within the organizational context of hospitals, however, doctors and nurses commonly treat patients like objects in need of fixing. As a consequence, the patient ceases to be a person and is treated much like an automobile at a repair shop (Goffman 1961). The same sometimes holds true for students at colleges. Professors and administrators commonly define students as objects to be processed, rather than as individual people with unique needs. I know of one professor, for instance, who fails any student who misses more than three classes per semester, regardless of the student's excuses or grades.

According to Goffman (1961), mental hospitals are designed for efficiency. As a consequence, patients are fed according to rigorous schedules, bedtimes and rising times are strictly enforced, and a variety of other standardized procedures are instituted. Those patients who are late risers, or who like food at odd hours, must accommodate themselves to the hospital's schedule. These practices developed out of hospital administrators' desire to create bureaucratic efficiency. Interestingly, these policies are also redefined by hospital staff as being essential components of patient treatment. Strict programming of the day's activities, for instance, is legitimated as a necessary means of teaching the mentally ill "responsibility" and "dependability." These **glorifying myths** are commonplace in bureaucracies and legitimize treating people in a variety of demeaning ways. Employees of colleges also produce glorifying myths. For example, the professor with the strict attendance policy defines her actions as something that she does *for* her students, not to her students. She believes that if she does not rigorously enforce her attendance policy, her students will not learn to be responsible individuals. Of course, it is entirely possible that students miss her classes because her lectures are of little value or because of unique circumstances that arise in their lives. Rather than questioning the reason for student absences, the professor produces a glorifying myth that legitimates her policy.

Bureaucracies also shape people to behave in peculiar ways and to have distorted values. Some workers develop an excessive commitment to rules and procedures, even when those rules and procedures get in the way of accomplishing organizational goals or treating people with dignity and respect. Robert Merton (1968) argued that these traits are evidence of a **bureaucratic personality.** He suggested that exposure to bureaucratic rationality can warp people into petty narrow-minded rule followers. The professor, with her attendance policy, has some of the characteristics of a bureaucratic personality. Her inflexible reaction to a breach of a rule, even when she is in a position to circumvent that rule, indicates a form of mental pathology. The unfortunate consequence of living and working in a bureaucratic society is that people sometimes feel their only sense of control is linked to the rules that they can enforce. They lose a sense that rules are here to serve people, and mistakenly assume that people are here to serve rules.

The Limits of Impersonality

Weber's ideal type posits that behavior in a bureaucracy is largely scripted by the formal rules. Thinking of how an industrial workplace might operate with bureaucratic efficiency, one would anticipate observing workers diligently laboring at a breakneck pace at isolated stations. Studies of worker behavior in factories, however, reveal that workers spend a considerable amount of time socializing and playing practical jokes on each other throughout the workday (Tulin 1984). If colleges operated like Weber's ideal type of bureaucracy, college life would primarily revolve around faculty and students spending their workdays disseminating and absorbing information for the sake of teaching and learning. In reality, a considerable proportion of the day is filled with gossip, idle conversation, and "goofing off." These observations reveal that people involved in bureaucracies engage in a great deal of social activity that has very little to do with organizational efficiency.

To explain this finding, organizational sociologists make a distinction between formal and informal relationships. Bureaucracies are designed to promote **formal relationships**—social attachments determined by organizational rules of conduct. **Informal relationships** are personal in nature and are characterized by a lack of formalized rules. Contrary to Weber's ideal type bureaucracy, studies of actual bureaucracies consistently reveal the importance of informal relationships within these organizations. One apparent conclusion is that people have a natural tendency to develop social arrangements that enable them to establish a sense of personal connection with other people. They will persistently do this in organizations that discourage interpersonal commitment because it counteracts the dehumanizing aspects of bureaucratic legal-rational authority.

In some respects, informal groups can actually expedite bureaucratic efficiency. Personal relations can be used in times of need to cut through red tape and can help other members maneuver around the sometimes onerous bureaucratic regulations. In other circumstances, informal groups are shown to detract from organizational efficiency. I know of one professor, for instance, who spends the bulk of his workday socializing with students, administrative assistants, secretaries, and other professors. His activities intrude on their ability to maximize production, but few complain because he helps brighten their day. In what could be a dehumanizing organizational structure, his informal relationships help break the drudgery that characterizes much of bureaucratic work.

Informal relationships are incredibly important to students in college society. Not only do they make study breaks enjoyable, they also provide networks for opportunity. Unfortunately, these networks of opportunity are not equally open to all members of college society. As C. Wright Mills (1978) observed, there are actually two Harvards, two Yales, and two Princetons. In each of these bureaucracies, there are clubs and cliques for students coming from old money and prestigious backgrounds. Students from less-privileged backgrounds are less likely to attain membership in these cliques and their informal relationships will tend to be with other students coming from similar class backgrounds. As a consequence, they will be less apt to form contacts with those individuals who are most likely to experience the greatest success later in life.

Informal relationships tend to undermine the principle of impartiality and fairness in bureaucracies. Studies reveal, for instance, that informal relationships greatly influence managers' decisions to favor their close friends, sometimes to the detriment of organizational efficiency and profitability (Kanter 1977). One particularly poignant example of this tendency is the practice of bequeathing "golden parachutes" to high-level managers when their employment is terminated. Obviously, when a person is fired or quits a job, they are no longer in a strong position to influence that organization's success. As a consequence, a rational organizational response would be to terminate compensation along with employment. This is usually the case when a low-level employee is laid off; the organization tends to offer little or nothing in terms of readjustment compensation (Barlett and Steele 1992). However, at the highest levels of management, golden parachutes are sometimes bestowed on departing administrators. I'll offer only two striking examples of the irrationality of this practice, one from private industry and one from academia.

In 1998, Sunbeam Corporation fired its CEO, Al Dunlap, for financial mismanagement. Dunlap had acquired the nickname "Chainsaw Al" for laying off thousands of employees at various corporations he had headed prior to working for Sunbeam. While most of these employees received little or no compensation when their jobs were terminated, Al Dunlap negotiated a handsome severance package estimated at $35 million (*Washington Post* 1998). In a strikingly similar scenario, Peter Diamandopoulos was fired from being president of Adelphi College in 1997. At the time of his termination, he was the second-highest-paid college president in the nation, earning $523,636 yearly in salary and benefits. Under his tenure, enrollment declined, tuition increased substantially, and fund-raising declined (*New York Times* 1998a). Upon termination, Diamandopoulos demanded that he be re-employed as a tenured professor (as is common for administrators who return to teaching) at 9/11ths of his base salary, $270,614 per year (*New York Times* 1998b). In the end, both Dunlap and Diamandopoulos had to settle for lower but still substantial compensation, but only after considerable press attention focused on the disproportionately lucrative packages offered to these departing executives. Why would a company or college offer golden parachutes to its departing high executives, but not to members in its lower ranks? One possible explanation is that high-level executives are in a position to form informal relationships with people who have the power to bequeath lucrative severance packages. Those at the lower end of the organizational hierarchy also form informal relationships, but these tend to be with others who lack power within the organization.

The Dysfunctionality of Hierarchy

Bureaucracies promote hierarchy, and thus create gulfs that separate workers from management. It is in the age of the scientific management, for instance, that a clear distinction emerges between blue collar workers and white collar workers. According to Richard Edwards (1979), these hierarchies contribute to conflict in the workplace, which he describes as a zone of contested terrain. As an illustration of Edward's argument, consider the consequences of instituting scientific management. Under the new system of scientific management, a strong class division emerged between workers and managers. Workers soon understood that cooperation with management's time studies would ultimately result in speedups and increased quotas, but not necessarily increased wages. As a means of resistance, workers pressured each other to refuse to work when directly observed, to work slowly when observation was unavoidable, and sometimes to sabotage machinery. Workers would also engage in meaningless activities in order to give an impression of working hard while actually not working at all (Montgomery 1979). Ultimately, it was the resistance to the new bureaucratic order that prompted many groups of workers to form labor unions, which enabled them to influence the rules of production and compensation.

Interestingly, workers learned that one of the best ways to fight managers was to use bureaucracy to their advantage. One particularly cagey strategy workers found to protest a speedup or cut in pay was to engage in a "work to rule" strike. Because bureaucracies develop increasing numbers of rules over time, eventually the rules themselves become a barrier to efficiency. Understanding this, workers learned that they could slow production to a crawl by following each bureaucratic rule to the letter. Because this form of protest involves following rules, rather than breaking them, there is little threat to any individual worker being fired for insubordination under the system, based on legal-rational authority.

Academia is a zone of contested terrain as well. Each college and university has a limited amount of financial resources and administrators are keen on maximizing faculty productivity for the least cost possible. Faculty are largely interested in maximizing their compensation and keeping their committee and coursework obligations to a minimum. Near the bottom of the organizational ladder are graduate students, the rough equivalent of modern-day apprentices. But perhaps the definition of graduate students as apprentices is a glorifying myth to describe the training of present-day graduate students, who are often required to teach their own classes or perform repetitious dirty work (grading) for faculty members.

Acting much like working-class employees in the early twentieth century, graduate teaching assistants at Yale engaged in a strike in 1995. Declaring that they were workers, not apprentices, the graduate students demanded improvements in their work conditions, benefits, and compensation. Understanding Yale's need to process student grades, the graduate students chose to strike at a critical time in the academic year, immediately following finals. Because many graduate students were responsible for keeping track of undergraduate student grades, their refusal to surrender grade books made it impossible for Yale to distribute accurate grade reports (Leatherman 1999).

Two lessons can be drawn from the graduate student strike at Yale. The first lesson is that bureaucratic rationality does not necessarily lead to liberation for all members of an organization. The reason why Yale does not pay its graduate students a higher wage is not because it cannot afford to. It can (Nelson 1977). In a quest for efficiency and productivity at a low cost, university administrators choose to offer its lesser-powered employees low compensation. Defining graduate students as "apprentices" rather than "workers" was a means of legitimating this decision. The second lesson is that bureaucracies can be brought to a grinding halt by dissatisfied workers. The response of Yale students is much like the response of workers laboring in bureaucracies in the twentieth century. Both groups figured out ways of paralyzing productivity by strategically targeting aspects of bureaucratic organization.

The Dysfunctionality of Specialization

Bureaucracies achieve efficiency through specialization, but critical sociologists point out that specialization is accompanied by a number of costs. Scientific management, for example, ultimately involves reducing worker's tasks to simple rudimentary procedures. While this organizational practice expedites production, it comes at a tremendous cost to workers, whose jobs become boring, repetitious, and unenjoyable. Karl Marx predicted this aspect of capitalist production with his concept of **alienation,** a term he used to describe the separation of workers from their natural creative inclinations (Tucker 1972). Marx believed that people are naturally creative and, if unconstrained, will work together to advance their collective interests. However, modern industrial practices create workplaces where jobs become little more than drudgery, warping the mind to believe that work is something to be avoided. Thus, Marx predicted that, in the modern workplace, workers would feel little connection with what they were making, little connection with coworkers, and little connection with their own creative potentials.

Deskilling of work also leads to impoverishment, a point forcefully argued in Harry Braverman's (1974) classic *Labor and Monopoly Capital.* Braverman posited that scientific management was designed not just for efficiency, but also to wrestle power away from the working class and place power in the hands of managers and owners. Scientific management creates a system that makes each individual worker replaceable. As a consequence, Braverman argued, workers lose their ability to assert their will in determining working conditions and their wages deteriorate as the demands for productivity increase. Viewed in this way, deskilling work is as much about control over corporate profits as it is about efficiency. Compare, for instance, the working conditions of people who make their living repairing automobiles. A skilled mechanic, who can diagnose and remedy a variety of automotive problems, is able to command a high wage. On the other hand, the oil changer employed at a Jiffy Lube (a deskilled job) earns a much lower wage. Because the Jiffy Lube employees are more easily replaced than mechanics, they must be satisfied with lower compensation.

As discussed above, college teaching has been deskilled in a number of respects. The difference between a college professor and a college instructor is remarkably similar to the difference between a mechanic and an oil changer. Professors are responsible for a wide range of activities, including curriculum development, research, publishing, teaching, advising, committee work, and grant writing. As a consequence, the job of a college professor requires a skilled and dedicated employee. In contrast, college instructors are usually expected to do only one task, teach specific courses. Remember that much of the material for lower-division college courses is prepackaged, and it is entirely possible for people with only a rudimentary understanding of their discipline to successfully teach a course. One of my former undergraduate sociology students, for instance, was employed at a nationally recognized university as a sociology instructor immediately after receiving her bachelor's degree. For the growing numbers of academics trapped in instructor jobs, earning a living often requires working at multiple colleges and working long hours for little pay. Increasing proportions of students are now taught by inexperienced or burned-out instructors, laboring for as little as $1500 per course (Nelson 1997; New York Times 1997).

There is another cost to specialization that warrants attention as well. The role of the specialist is to know a great deal about a very restricted area of concern. Current college employment practices promote faculty who have restricted interests and who focus on very narrowly defined problems. For example, universities no longer seek "scientists" or even "biologists"; instead they seek experts in behavioral genetics, or other highly specialized fields. While students have the benefit of brief exposure to experts, they are less likely to have contact with scholars conversant in the types of broad overarching knowledge that makes it possible to connect the various disciplines with one another. Modern social arrangements tend to discourage bridging of one discipline with another. It was only after the atom bomb was constructed, for instance, that scientists reflected on the sociopolitical consequences of their invention. During the construction, they were consumed primarily with an technical puzzles of designing this weapon (Oppenheimer 1989). To engage in such reflection would have required attention to a generalized knowledge of politics, history, and philosophy—subjects that the physicists' jobs discouraged.

According to Macedo (1994), many academics can be described as "learned ignoramuses." As a point of illustration, he tells of a graduate student researcher in linguistics at the Massachusetts Institute of Technology who had never heard of pidgin English. He wondered how a specialist in linguistics could be completely ignorant of a major dialect resulting from the historical fusion of cultures in the southern United States. He further wondered why, when this person was confronted with this ignorance, she seemed completely unconcerned, and in fact took pride in not distracting herself with something that she perceived as peripheral to her specialization in "theoretical linguistics." His observations may not be that unusual. Specialization can lead to a very peculiar form of expertise, producing disconnected groups of people, each knowing a great deal about surprisingly little.

McDonaldization of Society

According to Ritzer (1996), the success of many companies can be attributed to the same types of Taylorized-bureaucratic-mass-production processes used in fast-food restaurants such as McDonald's. Companies such as WalMart, Jiffy Lube, and LensCrafters adhere to the same organizational and technological practices that McDonald's uses with great success. In his analysis of these types of companies, Ritzer concludes that their success centers on organizational practices devoted to four overarching values: efficiency, calculability, predictability, and control. **McDonaldization** is simply a term used to conceptualize the social consequences of these values, values that are shaped by bureaucratization, mass production, and scientific management.

There is plenty to appreciate in a McDonald's. Service is prompt, the food is comparably inexpensive, and the restaurants are usually clean. Like other bureaucracies, McDonald's strives to be *efficient*. Toward this end, it seeks to use resources effectively. For example, McDonald's serves hamburgers and french fries because these items submit themselves to standardized cooking practices and will satisfy a large proportion of customers. Eating food at a McDonald's does not require the use of utensils, and by offering mostly finger foods, McDonald's can forgo the expense of plates, knives, forks, and spoons. Consider also that at a McDonald's not only is the food prepared on assembly lines, but customers are also processed on assembly lines as well (Ritzer 1996).

Critical thinking reveals a number of costs to this efficiency. For example, while customers can expect food quickly, they are required to do much of the work involved, such as queuing up to the counters, carrying trays, and disposing of garbage. Workers engaged in unskilled and alienating work get little enjoyment, no skill development, and scant monetary reward from their labor. Quality suffers as well, because food is prepared not with an eye toward nutrition or taste, but rather toward maximizing shelf life under the heat lamps. To understand Ritzer's point here (if you are not a vegetarian), go to a McDonald's, order a hamburger, and seriously look at it and taste it. See how well it compares with a homemade hamburger prepared on a grill.

Of course, college campus cafeterias now operate using McDonald's' principles of production. But beyond this, McDonaldized efficiency is creeping into other areas of campus life. College students are processed by financial aid officers in much the same way customers are treated at a McDonald's, and are commonly expected to shuttle papers from office to office. Is it possible that students are the rough equivalent of hamburgers in the eyes of university administrators and professors? If this is true, the value of efficiency may displace the value placed on quality. Consider, for example, the widespread practice of grading students by multiple-choice tests. Any reasonable individual will conclude that, in comparison to other evaluation techniques (such as essay or oral exams), these tests do a poor job. However, if the goal is to evaluate many students quickly, multiple-choice tests are valued.

Calculability refers to the value placed on understanding the world in terms of numerical facts. For example, McDonald's describes its food with words connoting size, such as "big," "supersize," or "value," and illusions of size are carefully constructed using deceptive packaging. Signs at McDonald's post how many billions of people have been served. Calculability is also evidenced in the entertainment business. For example, television producers use Nielsen ratings to assess television show popularity and news shows examine box-office draws to gauge a movie's merits. On the surface, calculability appears rational, but it can lead to very irrational results. One consequence of a cultural embrace of calculability is the equating of size with quality. A Quarter Pounder with cheese and a supersize order of french fries and a small shake, for instance, seems like a bargain. From a nutritional perspective, though, this is questionable, in that this meal would provide 116% of the daily requirement of saturated fat and 79% of the recommended consumption of sodium (McDonald's Nutrition Facts 1999; Ritzer 1996).

College life is increasingly guided by the values of calculability. For instance, grade point averages (GPAs) reduce student academic success to a single numerical indicator. The heavy reliance on the grade point average produces some very irrational results. For instance, understanding that a bad grade can pull down a GPA, intelligent students make decisions to avoid difficult courses. Understanding that challenging professorial authority can result in a lower course grade, students also tend to avoid conflict and do their work with an eye toward conformity rather than creativity (see Bowles and Gintis 1976). In practice, the GPA works to motivate students to work for their grades rather than for their education.

Professors are also influenced by calculability. Consider, for instance, how teaching evaluations are performed. Typically students evaluate professors on scantron forms, rating their teaching on scales of 1 to 5 (excellent to poor). These surveys are later processed into summary tables of percentages, indicating an overall evaluation of the professor. On the surface this appears rational, but it can lead to irrational consequences. Professors, for instance, may start teaching with an eye toward increasing their popularity and as a consequence neglect demanding students' best work. In this quest for popularity, there is a strong temptation to sacrifice course content for jokes and entertaining anecdotes (Edmundson 1997).

Administrators commonly use "FTE" calculations to determine budgetary allotments to departments and campuses. FTE stands for "full-time equivalent," and it represents the number of full-time students per faculty member. The greater the FTE, the greater the perceived productivity of a department or a college. Within the State University of New York system, for example, the amount of money given to individual campuses is prorated in terms of each individual campus' FTE statistic. Those campuses with higher FTEs receive more money from the state than colleges with low FTEs. Unfortunately, this system ignores the fact that some campuses and some disciplines require smaller student-to-faculty ratios. Remote rural campuses will be limited in their ability to attract students, and therefore will be at a disadvantage in comparison to urban campuses. Campuses that offer programs that involve heavy student/faculty contact, such as music performance, are also penalized under such a system. As campuses think about competing for increasingly scarce resources, they are pressured to focus on programs that will be low-cost and highly popular. The unfortunate result of calculating program worth on the basis of head counts is that courses and programs that do not generate FTEs, such as the arts, are devalued. Calculability leads to the conclusion that popularity can be equated with value. As Plato diagnosed in *The Republic,* in the field of education this assumption is highly questionable.

Predictability is the value placed upon using past experience to determine the efficacy of future activities. McDonald's, for instance, only rarely introduces a new product because its existing menu has proved so successful in the past. Hollywood also uses its past successes to determine its future activities, as evidenced in its heavy reliance on sequels. Using the "tried-and-true" method of planning future activities leads to irrational consequences, though. Directors and recording artists are pushed to create already familiar products and the entertainment industry offers scant support for experimental or innovative work (see Becker 1982). As a consequence, convention rather than innovation is promoted in artistic production. In college society, professors rely on conventional classroom teaching techniques because these offer predictable results on student evaluations. Comparably few teachers risk using innovative pedagogical approaches because these experiments run the risk of lowering course evaluations. As a consequence, faculty tend to avoid new teaching techniques that could potentially bring higher levels of excitement and productivity to classroom encounters (Sweet 1998).

Possibly the most poignant illustration of the irrationality of calculability and predictability in academia can be illustrated by the heavy reliance on the standardized Aptitude Test. The SAT was designed to assess students' "aptitudes," the degree to which they possess the necessary qualities that will insure likely success at the college level. The test involves a multiple-choice examination of verbal ability and mathematical ability. Students receive separate scores for both sections of the test, but these scores can be combined into a single SAT score, the maximum being 1600 points. These scores provide an easy means for admissions officers to rank their college's applicants.

On the surface, the SAT appears to be a rational and fair system of evaluating student applicants, but there are a number of problems with the SAT. One major concern is that it ignores students' knowledge of history, social studies, art, science, and technology. Another concern is that it does not offer any indication of a student's social skills or motivation. It also discriminates against students coming from underprivileged school districts who may have had poor educational opportunities but who could thrive in an enriched college environment. But probably the most serious concern with the SAT is that *it is actually a very weak predictor of college success.*

The SAT can be reliably used in order to compare the likely success of students scoring very high on the exam (~1400) in comparison to students scoring very low on the exam (~500). It isn't surprising that the very high scoring students have a much higher likelihood of college success than the very low scoring students. What the SAT cannot do is predict the likelihood of success of students with modest differences in their scores. This is the problem. In practice, the SAT is used to make comparisons between students with small to moderate differences in their scores. For instance, administrators assume that the student scoring 1400 on the SAT is a vastly better candidate than the student who scores 1200. The SAT, however, is extremely bad at predicating student success based on such comparatively small differences in test scores. In terms of statistical probabilities of success in college, there is little or no difference between a student scoring 1400 and a student scoring 1200 on the SAT (Berline and Biddle 1997; Lemann 1995).

McDonaldization is also guided by values asserting the desirability of *control*. The value placed on control is reflected in a desire to eliminate individual discretion or variation in the workplace. Companies such as McDonald's increasingly try to control their workers through the use of technology. Cash registers, for instance, are designed to calculate change, fryers have timers programmed to cook fries, dispensers regulate the filling of cups, etc. Colleges are following McDonald's lead and are increasingly using technology to regulate social relations. Scantron tests, for instance, remove some of the professorial discretion in determining student grades. Administrators use teaching evaluations to control professors and make them accountable for classroom performance.

It is entirely possible that technology can replace many professorial positions in the foreseeable future. Professors can be undependable and demanding. There are distinct advantages to developing new technologies to control (or eliminate) these potential troublemakers. The fact that textbook companies now refer to themselves as "information providers" may be a harbinger of the demise of the professor. In the brave new classroom, lecture material may be embedded into CD-ROMs. Students could be evaluated at computer terminals as they respond to preprogrammed batteries of questions. Perhaps the entire physical college can be dispensed with, as is the case with Phoenix University, a college that literally has no campus (Traub 1997).

Discussion: Coping with the Iron Cage

We are now living in a world dominated by bureaucracies and legal-rational authority. Not only are colleges run according to bureaucratic principles, but so are hospitals, corporations, and governments. Max Weber accurately predicted that these organizations would make it possible to live in an efficient society, capable of performing the complex services needed in the modern world. He also predicted the emergence of the dark, dehumanizing effects of bureaucracy, a world where the impersonal rule-driven encounters would trap people in the "**iron cage of rationality**." Weber believed that as society increasingly relies on legal-rational authority, people would be ever more constrained and estranged from one another by the hierarchies, divisions of labor, and impersonal rules imposed by bureaucracies.

The degree to which we are, or will be, trapped in an iron cage is questionable. I believe, or at least sincerely hope, that students, faculty, and administrators will continue to interact with one another on a much more personal level than Weber predicted. But I also believe that if we are nonreflective, if we don't think about how we want society to operate, the walls of the cage will continue to be built. The concluding question concerns how to fight the irrational consequences of bureaucratization. What strategies will structure a society that takes advantage of the positive features of bureaucracy, while at the same time minimizing the dehumanizing consequences that seem to emerge from this organizational form?

Studies of labor history reveal that people will not necessarily be passive victims of bureaucracy. Members of the working class in the automotive industries, for example, responded to deskilling and issues of declining job security by unionizing and engaging in collective bargaining (Montgomery 1979; Shaiken 1984). As a consequence of occasional strikes, workers in the automobile industry were able to obtain high wages and job security even in a deskilled work environment. This suggests that human control can exert a tremendous influence on charting the path of history. Of course, unions produced new problems, but in a number of ways they proved highly effective at preventing some of the problems that, left unchecked, would have likely arisen (Heckscher 1988). History will tell if graduate students at Yale will be able to achieve similar benefits through similar tactics, and if they do, what consequences it will have on the experience of higher education.

When technological development has corresponded with a desire to control people through inventions like the assembly line, the intrinsic rewards of working have declined. Technology studies reveal, however, that technologies can be produced that liberate rather than constrain workers and that these alternative approaches will not necessarily impinge on productivity (Noble 1979). As a point of illustration, consider how the word processor is a liberating technology for professors and students, enabling them to engage in desktop publishing. This involves a variety of skills including writing, editing, graphics, and page composing. On the other hand, word processors for clerical workers contribute to job dissatisfaction and subject them to further control. Laboring all day in a typing pool is not only alienating, it also can produce carpal tunnel syndrome, a physically debilitating condition. The same technology that makes it possible for me to write this book also enables companies to count the words processed by clerical workers. In reality it is a social choice to use technology to deskill and control people, or to use technology as a means of stimulating and promoting creativity (Howard 1985; Shaiken 1984).

There are a number of irrational consequences of the bureaucratization and Taylorization of college life. Is it possible to counteract some of these processes? Suppose, for instance, a professor chooses to evaluate her students with multiple-choice exams. Does that mean that her students have to submit themselves to this exam structure? What would happen if students engaged in the same types of sabotaging activities early industrial workers used when faced with the assembly line. This could be done easily enough by filling the exams out in pen, tearing small nicks in the edges of the exam, or writing answers in longhand on blank pieces of paper. Perhaps another strategy would suffice. For those students who consistently do poorly on multiple-choice tests, it seems reasonable that their institutions honor requests to allow them an exam in a different format. Organizationally, these students would be comparable to the customer at a McDonald's who wants a hamburger without catsup. If the requests are founded on rational grounds, organizations can be forced to make accommodations even if those accommodations disrupt the normal bureaucratic procedures.

To a great extent, the shape of bureaucratic society depends on human decisions. Left unchecked, the desire for efficiency results in dehumanizing practices. At the same time, treating each person as a unique individual undermines the processes that make it possible to serve many people in a cost-effective manner. The quest for rationality is probably inherently coupled with processes that have the potential to dehumanize and estrange people from one another. Serious reflection on organizational dynamics will hopefully enable truly rational choices, even if these decisions entail some cost to organizational efficiency. As William H. Whyte (1956) pointed out, the organization man has the potential to reshape the bureaucracy, using it advance lives and society beyond narrowly defined terms of economic gain. This will occur, though, only through vigilance and attentive reflection to the role bureaucracy plays in modern life.

REFERENCES

Bailyn, Bernard. 1986. "Foundations" in Bailyn, Bernard, Donald Fleming, Oscar Handlin, and Stephan Thernstrom, *Glimpses of the Harvard Past*. Cambridge, MA: Harvard University Press.

Bailyn, Bernard. 1986. "Why Kirkland Failed" in Bailyn, Bernard, Donald Fleming, Oscar Handlin, and Stephan Thernstrom, *Glimpses of the Harvard Past*. Cambridge: Harvard University Press.

Barlett, Donald and James Steele. 1992. *America: What Went Wrong?* Kansas City: Andrews and McMeel.

Battles, Matthew. 2000. "Lost in the Stacks." *Harpers*. January: 36–39.

Becker, Howard, B. Geer, E. C. Hughes, and A. Straus. 1961. *Boys in White: Student Culture in Medical School*. Chicago: University of Chicago Press.

Becker, Howard. 1982. *Art Worlds*. Berkeley: University of California Press.

Berline, David and Bruce Biddle. 1997. *The Manufactured Crisis: Myths, Fraud, and the Attack on America's Public Schools*. New York: Longman.

Blau, Peter and Marshall Meyer. 1987. *Bureaucracy in Modern Society*. New York: Random House.

Bowles, Samuel and Herbert Gintis. 1976. *Schooling in Capitalist America: Educational Reform and the Contradictions of Economic Life*. New York: Basic Books.

Braverman, Harry. 1974. *Labor and Monopoly Capital*. New York: Monthly Review Press.

Burowoy, Michael. 1979. *Manufacturing Consent: Changes in the Labor Process Under Monopoly Capitalism*. Chicago: University of Chicago Press.

Chandler, Alfred. 1990. *Scale and Scope: The Dynamics of Industrial Capitalism.* Cambridge, MA: Belknap Press.

Edmundson, Mark. 1997. "On the Uses of a Liberal Education: I. As Lite Entertainment for Bored College Students." *Harper's* September. 295:39–49.

Edwards, Richard. 1979. *Contested Terrain: The Transformation of the Workplace in the Twentieth Century.* New York: Basic Books.

Foucault, Michel. 1977. *Discipline and Punish: The Birth of the Prison.* New York: Pantheon.

Gerth, H. H. and C. Wright Mills [eds]. 1946. *From Max Weber: Essays in Sociology.* New York: Oxford University Press.

Goffman, Erving. 1961. *Asylums: Essays on the Social Situation of Mental Patients and Other Inmates.* Garden City, New York: Doubleday

Handlin, Oscar. 1986. "Making Men of Boys" in Bailyn, Bernard, Donald Fleming, Oscar Handlin, and Stephan Thernstrom, *Glimpses of the Harvard Past.* Cambridge: Harvard University Press.

Heckscher, Charles. 1988. *The New Unionism: Employee Involvement in the Changing Corporation.* New York: Basic Books.

Howard, Robert. 1985. *Brave New Workplace.* New York: Viking.

Kanter, Rosabeth Moss. 1977. *Men and Women of the Corporation.* New York: Basic Books.

Lemann, Nicholas. 1995. "The Great Sorting." *Atlantic Monthly.* 276:84–98.

Leatherman, Courtney. 1999. "Decision in Yale Case Leaves Graduate Students and University Both Claiming Victory." *Chronicle of Higher Education.* Pg. A20

Marshall, Ray and Marc Tucker. 1992. *Thinking for a Living: Education and the Wealth of Nations.* New York: Basic Books.

Macedo, Donaldo. 1994. *Literacies of Power: What Americans Are Not Allowed to Know.* Boulder: Westview.

McDonald's Nutrition Facts. 1999. *http://www.mcdonalds.com/food/nutrition/*

Merton, Robert. 1968. "Bureaucratic Structure and Personality" in *Social Theory and Social Structure,* 3rd ed. New York: Free Press.

Mills, C. Wright. 1978. *The Power Elite.* New York: Oxford University Press.

Montgomery, David. 1979. *Workers' Control in America: Studies in the History of Work, Technology, and Labor Struggles.* Cambridge: Cambridge University Press.

Morrison, Samuel Eliot. 1936. *Three Centuries of Harvard, 1636–1936.* Cambridge: Harvard University Press.

Nelson, Cary. 1997. *Manifesto of a Tenured Radical.* New York: New York University Press.

New York Times. 1997. "The End of Tenure?" June 29, pp. 4–14

New York Times. 1998. "President Who Was Forced from Job at Adelphi Is Hired at Boston University." December 6, pp. 58.

New York Times. 1998. "Dismissed Head of Adelphi Asks to Teach, For $270,000." March 7, pp. 1.

Noble, David. 1979. *America by Design: Science, Technology, and the Rise of Corporate Capitalism.* New York: Alfred Knopf.

Oppenheimer, Robert. 1989. *Atom and Void: Essays on Science and Community.* Princeton, NJ: Princeton University Press.

Plato. 1987. *The Republic.* New York: Penguin.

Ritzer, George. 1996. *The McDonaldization of Society.* Thousand Oaks, CA: Pine Forge Press.

Rosovsky, Henry. 1990. *The University: An Owner's Manual.* New York: W. W. Norton.

Shaiken, Harley. 1984. *Work Transformed: Automation and Labor in the Computer Age.* New York: Holt, Reinhart and Winston.

Sweet, Stephen. 1998. "Practicing Radical Pedagogy: Balancing Ideals with Institutional Constraints." *Teaching Sociology.* 26:100–111.

Taylor, Frederick Winslow. 1964 [1911]. *The Principles of Scientific Management.* New York: Harper.

Thernstrom, Stephan. 1986. "Poor but Hopeful Scholars" in Bailyn, Bernard, Donald Fleming, Oscar Handlin, and Stephan Thernstrom [eds.]. *Glimpses of the Harvard Past*. Cambridge: Harvard University Press.

Thompson, E. P. 1967. "Time, Work-Discipline, and Industrial Capitalism." *Past and Present*. 38:56–97.

Traub, James. 1997. "Drive-Thru U." *The New Yorker* 73:144–153.

Trumpbour, John. 1989. "Introducing Harvard: A Social, Philosophical and Political Profile" in Trumpbour, John [ed.] *How Harvard Rules*. Boston: South End Press.

Tucker, Robert. 1972. *The Marx-Engels Reader*. New York: Norton.

Tulin, Roger. 1984. *A Machinist's Semi-Automated Life*. San Pedro: Singlejack Books.

Washington Post. 1998. "From Charlton to 'Chainsaw.'" June 25, page B2.

Weissman, Robert. 1989. "How Harvard Is Ruled: Administration and Governance at the Corporate University" in Trumpbour, John [ed.] *How Harvard Rules*. Boston: South End Press.

Whyte, William H. 1956. *The Organization Man*. New York: Simon and Schuster.

5 College Athletics, Cohesion, and Exploitation

One of the most important tenets underpinning the sociological imagination is that different parts of society operate according to common principles. One illustration of this insight is that even though individuals making up organizations may be different, these organizations function in remarkably similar ways. For example, individual players and coaches vary at different universities, but the football teams at places like Notre Dame, Duke, and Syracuse all do similar things in the locker rooms and on the field. Likewise, although the fans may root for different teams, the way they cheer their team will only vary in the most modest ways. To make this bridge from team to team, or fan to fan, requires only a limited use of the sociological imagination.

To truly think like a sociologist is to comprehend similarities in the operations of very different parts of society. The sociological imagination involves creating parallels between different cultures and the common purposes those social institutions have within each society. For example, is it possible to link what happens in a college hockey game at Cornell University and a cockfight in Bali? To expand the sociological imagination even further requires linking very different social institutions with one another. For example, in what ways do sports and religion contribute to the systemic operations of society?

Sports, for amateurs, comprise for a pastime. For spectators, sports are a form of entertainment. For the select few who become professional athletes, sports can be a vocation. One thing is clear, though: sports are anything but trivial social events, given the financial stakes in athletics and the great deal of attention they receive. From a sociological perspective, these are events worthy of serious inquiry, but what exactly is the role of sports in society?

One important question concerns why some types of sports are popular in some cultures, yet have little appeal in other cultures. For instance, why are sports such as football, hockey, and basketball so popular on American campuses, but other sports less popular? To answer this question requires comparing different cultures and observing the ways in which particular sports resonate with dominant cultural values and concerns. Such questions require comparative analysis, examining the differences and similarities of an institution in societies that have very different cultures. As an introduction to the sociology of sports, let us take a journey halfway around the world, to Bali, a small island in Indonesia, and examine the role sports play in that society. Then, we will make a return journey and look at the role sports play on American college campuses, using a similar analytic approach.

Sports as Reflective of Culture

Few Balinese know much about American contact sports. Lacking this knowledge, few Balinese can appreciate the level of excitement Cornell students experience while watching a Big Red player body slam one of Clarkson's Golden Knights into the boards. Nor do the Balinese appreciate the drama of seeing a goalie leave his box in order to create an opportunity for a last-ditch effort for a tying goal in the final seconds of the game. Likewise, few Cornell students know much about cockfighting, even though it occurs in a small number of venues in the United States (Bilger 1999). As a consequence, they will be inclined to perceive this simply as a brutal blood sport, rather than appreciate the skill involved in training, matching, and pitting one rooster against another in a challenge to the death. I suspect that, in the eyes of some Balinese, Cornell students are experientially impoverished because they haven't fully realized the leap of the heart when a rooster, on the verge of death, makes one final thrust at its opponent to deliver a fatal blow.

One way of understanding the importance of sports such as hockey and cockfighting to society is to interpret them as **cultural performances,** dramatic representations of a society's norms and values (Cady 1978; Geertz 1973; Mason 1995). According to the anthropologist Clifford Geertz, the study of these types of events can be a key to understanding deeply held values of a society. As Geertz writes:

> As much of America surfaces in a ball park, on a golf links, at a race track, or around a poker table, much of Bali surfaces in a cock ring. (1973; 417)

Geertz's appraisal suggests that a serious analysis of comparatively trivial social events, such as a hockey tournament or a cockfight, may actually offer more information about a culture than would a detailed study of a notable trial, a public election, or even laws passed by governments. The concern for sociologists and anthropologists, following Geertz's lead, involves identifying the meaning of these events from the perspective of their participants and linking these events to the prevailing norms and values of their society. Because cockfighting and hockey are so enthusiastically received in their respective societies, they reveal important things about these very different cultures.

In his classic essay "Notes on the Balinese Cockfight," (1973) Geertz argues that sporting events, such as cockfights and hockey games, can be interpreted as a form of **deep play.** On the surface, these events appear to be diversions or simply opportunities to wager money. However, a more serious inquiry leads to the conclusion that they reveal core cultural values and assist in maintaining societal integrity. In reality, cockfighting is much more than simply a competition between roosters, it is a competition between people and represents the deep cultural beliefs about how Balinese society operates. The same holds true for sporting events at American universities.

Cornell is not Bali and Bali is not Cornell, but there are some obvious similarities between a cockfight and a hockey game. Both are fast-paced, occur in rings, draw large crowds, and the best competitions are the most closely matched. The most exciting contests tend also to be the bloodiest. Although it is tempting to extend an exhaustive list of parallels between the two events and argue that they are one and the same, this would require glossing over the many differences in the sports, as well as important differences in Balinese and American culture. For example, whereas Americans are commonly characterized as being aggressive, traditional Balinese culture asserts the desirability of avoiding conflict. For Americans, to be likened to an animal is often a compliment (i.e., "party animal," "foxy," "stud"). In Bali, to be compared with an animal is an insult and, in some circumstances, even constitutes a form of punishment. So intense is the Balinese concern of individuals appearing animalistic that babies are even discouraged from crawling (Geertz 1973). Another difference is that Bali approximates a unisex society and its citizens play down sexual differences between men and women in clothing and conduct (Geertz, 1973). In the United States, these differences are pervasively reinforced, as the popularity of John Gray's (1992) *Men Are from Mars, Women Are from Venus* franchise demonstrates. Just as there are cultural differences between Bali and the United States, these differences are reflected in the cockfight and in American-style contact sports.

Geertz's "Notes on the Balinese Cockfight" (1973) details the cockfight, first describing its processes and then the relevance to the larger social order of Balinese society. To stage a cockfight first involves carefully pairing two roosters for an equal match. These birds have been bred, nurtured, and systematically trained for the fight, so matching requires judging genetic legacy, as well as overall physical stature and aggressiveness of the birds. Once a match is made, razor-sharp spikes are affixed to the roosters' spurs, and peppers or other medicines are sometimes shoved into their anuses to bring out a fighting spirit. The roosters are then positioned facing each other in the center of a ring that measures approximately fifty square feet. A coconut with a small hole, is placed in a pail of water in order to gauge the time it takes the roosters to engage in battle. A slit gong is then struck signaling the start of the match. If the roosters do not fight by the time the coconut sinks, the handlers pick them up and tease them to a frenzy, and place them down again for another attempt at battle. If the cocks still refuse to fight, they are then placed together in a wicker cage until they begin fighting.

The first round of fighting continues until one rooster delivers a solid blow to the other cock, at which point the owner of the winning bird separates it from the losing bird. Haste is needed in this regard because, as the birds tussle about, the losing bird stands a good chance of returning a fatal blow. During the interval between rounds, the handler of the losing bird uses a variety of methods to re-instill life in the creature. This can include placing the bird's head in his mouth and sucking out the blood that has collected in the bird's lungs, or plying its wounds with ointments. The contest recommences after the coconut is sunk three times. The owner of the rooster that is still able to stand and fight is declared the winner of the match. The loser then relinquishes possession of his dead cock to the owner of the winning bird.

This event occurs amidst intense interest and gambling, the most serious of which occurs near the ring between the competing owners and their families at even money. In general, the bigger the bet in the center ring, the more interest will be accorded the match. There are a variety of norms regulating center ring bets. For instance, relatives never bet against another relative's bird. A different system of betting occurs in the outer periphery of the circle among the other spectators. These individuals place bets with one another through a conversation of hand gestures that enables them to negotiate odds for their wagers. The betting becomes most frantic just prior to the release of the birds. In Bali, an island where wages are very low, it is not unusual to observe people betting the equivalent of three or four days wages' on a single cockfight. Following the match, all bets are paid immediately.

Geertz observed that cockfighting is not just an idle pastime or hobby; it is a passion that consumes people:

> Balinese men, or anyway a large majority of Balinese men, spend an enormous amount of time with their favorites, grooming them, feeding them, discussing them, trying them out against one another, or just gazing at them with a mixture of rapt admiration and dreamy self-absorption. Whenever you see a group of Balinese men squatting idly in the council shed or along the road with their hips down, shoulders forward, knees up fashion, half or more of them will have a rooster in his hands, holding it between his thighs, bouncing it gently up and down to strengthen its legs, ruffling its feathers with abstract sensuality, pushing it out against a neighbor's rooster to rouse its spirit, withdrawing it toward his loins to calm it again. Now and then, to get a feel for another bird, a man will fiddle this way with someone else's cock for a while, but usually by moving

around to squat in place behind it, rather than just having it passed across to him as though it were merely an animal. (418–419)

Even if one has never read Freud, the significance of the rooster to Balinese men is obvious. The word "cock" has the same double meaning in Bali as it does in America, and Balinese men make the same types of phallus jokes that American men make. Clearly the cockfight is not really about roosters, it is about competitions between men in a society where such overt competitions are discouraged. The cocks represent these men's manhood and the competitions are actually competitions between men, not roosters. This explains the norms of betting, the amounts wagered, and the intense interest in the matches.

On the surface it seems odd that a culture that reviles animals and shuns conflict would delight in cockfighting, but according to Geertz the cockfight exists for this very reason. For Balinese society, a cockfight provides a socially sanctified venue that enables controlled social conflict and a means for members of Balinese society to release tensions stemming from personal, familial, and clan rivalries. Only when viewed from this perspective does the considerable amount of time, money, and energy put in the cockfighting enterprise become understandable. At its deepest level, the cockfight is a means for different factions in Balinese society to demonstrate their loyalties, engage in symbolic challenges to existing social hierarchies, and express otherwise socially prohibited animal sexuality.

If Geertz is correct about sports reflecting core culture values and norms, the same types of observations should be revealed in the deep play of American college contact sports such as hockey and football. Like the cockfight in Bali, college contact sports resonate with deeply held values in American society. Like the cockfight in Bali, contact sports reaffirm American beliefs concerning the individual's place in society and provide a means for individuals to integrate themselves into that social order. It also may offer some "safety valve" functions like the cockfight in Bali, enabling Americans to release tension and frustration.

One question concerns why some types of sports have greater appeal than others in American society. There are a wide variety of contact sports familiar to Americans, but only a few really captivate audiences. For instance, football and rugby are remarkably similar, but football is much more popular in America and rugby is more popular in Europe and Australia. It is interesting to note that the underlying premise of rugby and football is identical, and that both games developed from the game "Danes Head," played in the tenth and eleventh centuries. Danes Head was simply a competition between two different townships to kick a ball (some have speculated a skull or a cow's bladder) from one town to the next. Modern rugby matches remain similar to Danes Head, as two teams of undifferentiated players strive to transport an oblong ball across a goal line using superior brute force. Like Danes Head, one appeal of rugby is its relative absence of rules. In contrast, football involves a plethora of rules regarding what constitutes appropriate and illegal contact. Football is not so much about brute force as it is about skill, speed, and precision, used in harmony with tactics.

If the overarching premise of the games is so similar, and since Americans were exposed to rugby, why did Americans choose to develop the game to the new sport of football? According to Reisman and Denney (1971), rugby was modified because it did not coincide closely enough with the norms and values emerging in nineteenth-century America. As a form of deep play, football offers a representation of American society, corresponding with the interactional styles cultivated in the American workplace, reflecting the workers' relationships with other workers and managers.

The first intercollegiate football match occurred in 1869, between Rutgers (six goals) and Princeton (four goals). At this historical juncture, America had already begun to industrialize and shift from its agrarian roots. The emerging new "American system" of production placed a much lower priority on brute power (valued in farming labor) and placed a much higher value on systematic, rule-based styles of interaction (Chandler 1990). Industrialization required new ways of interacting, such as showing up at the workplace at prescheduled hours and laboring for long hours on rigidly defined tasks. Football reflected this style of interacting, re-creating on the field the styles of interacting already familiar to Americans in the workplace.

In the nineteenth century, Americans were also starting to appreciate the economic advantages in creating a high **division of labor.** Going fast were the days where an individual craftsman made a commodity, such as shoes, from start to finish. Industry was retooled and reorganized to produce consumer goods with workers occupying stations, performing small, repetitious subsidiary tasks. In the shoe industry, for instance, some workers tanned, others stitched, and others molded soles. Football mirrored this organizational strategy by dividing labor as well. Unlike the scrum in rugby, which involves an undifferentiated mob of players pushing and kicking for control of a ball, football requires that specific players occupy discrete positions such as quarterback, linebacker, and wide receiver. Football, perhaps more than any other sport, operates on a principle of division of labor. Consider, for example, the fact that a number of college teams recruit some players for no other purpose than simply to kick field goals.

Part of the popularity of contact sports may be attributable to the strong resonance these sports have with American beliefs concerning economic social relations. American brands of economic theory emphasize that competition is the key to social progress. Competition is seen as a positive and necessary part of social order, and it is believed to stimulate efficiency and inventiveness through a process of "creative destruction" (Schumpeter

1951/1989). Americans also believe that competition is a means of sorting people into their appropriate ranks in society. Contact sports offer a representation of this contest and reaffirm for Americans belief in the naturalness and social desirability of competition, as well as the notion that progress requires both inventiveness and aggression. In terms of deep play, these sports provide a venue where these deeply held beliefs are made visible in the form of individuals going head-to-head in battles over territory (Cady 1978).

Analysis of the formal rules of play in contact sports reveals other cultural themes that link people with one another. The response of fans and participants to these events, particularly in moments of intense passion, reveals much about the culture. For instance, the rules of hockey stipulate what one can and cannot do while attempting to get a puck into an opponent's goal. But for anyone who has ever observed a college hockey game, some of the most interesting events are the transgressions of those rules, such as when hockey players deliberately trip, slash, or slam each other even when the puck is nowhere in their vicinity. As shown poignantly in the film *Slap Shot*, much of the appeal of hockey for fans is simply the violence associated with the game.

When the rogue player slams an opponent hard into the boards, fans feel elated and cheer. One explanation for the excitement created by this violence may be that these violations represent the fans' animosity toward regulation of competitive social behavior. As noted by a number of social critics (i.e., Bellah et al. 1985; Galbraith 1976), Americans harbor deep resentment toward government intervention in their lives, even though this intervention oftentimes helps create clean drinking water, safe streets, and good schools. In that the hockey match is society played out in the arena, it offers fans a chance to see this perceived oppressive regulation subverted. It offers a cathartic experience to see the rules flaunted, if only in a rather fictive form. Even if this joy is brief, it may work as a safety valve, enabling fans to release tension stemming from perceived social constraints (Pearton 1986).

American contact sports also offer sexual parallels with Geertz's analysis of the Balinese cockfight. Recall that the cockfight provides an opportunity for the Balinese men to express desires in a socially acceptable manner. Intercollegiate contact sports may offer a similar function. There is a remarkable amount of physical contact between men in college contact sports, not only of the violent sort, but also intimate contract that is discouraged in almost all other encounters between men. Contact sports provide socially acceptable venues for men to express desires for male intimacy and to bond on an emotional level. By offering men a socially sanctified means of expressing this intimacy, sports strengthen the stability of society and help compensate for cultural restrictions on personal desires.

In summation, an anthropological analysis of the Balinese cockfight and college contact sports suggest that these games mirror the society as a whole, and thereby reflect deeply held cultural values and expectations about social conduct (Haerle 1974; Powers 1992). As a consequence, they instill and reinforce deeply held convictions about social order. They also provide a sort of "safety valve" and release frustrations or tensions concerning socially prohibited desires (Pearton 1986).

Sports and Cohesion

The above discussion highlights that sports offer a reflection of norms and values in society. Sports also perform vital functions in integrating people with one another, a purpose central to the well-being of society. To understand these processes, the analysis of sports can be reframed within a functionalist perspective, examining the ways in which sports facilitate the integration of individuals into the larger social order and the means by which sports contribute to social harmony.

Applying the functionalist perspective to social relations requires examining two issues—identification of universally important institutions and discerning the function or purpose of these institutions in society. Functionalist theorists have observed that all societies share common similar institutions, including governments, education systems, families, economies, and religions. The form of each institution varies from society to society (for example, economies may be communist, socialist, or capitalist), but because every society has an economic structure, the economic institutions are likely to be of great importance in keeping that society intact.

Sporting events constitute one of these institutions because almost all known societies have integrated competitive sports into their cultures in one form or another. While the sports themselves may vary from society to society (i.e., sumo wrestling, cockfighting, football), the presence of sports is ubiquitous. It is also interesting to observe that most colleges have integrated competitive sports into their organizations. The primary question for functionalists concerns why sports are present in society and identifying the vital functions that they fulfill.

The Manifest and Latent Functions of Sports

Functionalist analysis hinges on identifying the purposes institutions have in creating and maintaining the health of society. Answering this question requires differentiating between two different types of functions, manifest functions and latent functions. **Manifest functions** are the acknowledged, or taken-for-granted, purposes that a social institution has in society. For instance, a manifest function of colleges is to teach people the technical skills and the knowledge that will prepare them for entry into the world of work.

In the case of college sports, some manifest functions are the entertainment of fans, recreational opportunities for athletes, and the creation of physically fit citizens.

Identifying the **latent functions** of a social institution requires examining the unacknowledged or hidden roles that this institution plays in maintaining the health of society. For example, while it is acknowledged that colleges provide skills and knowledge to students that will later enable them to be effective employees, this function alone cannot justify the amount of time and expense invested in a college education. If colleges were just about teaching skills, this could be much more efficiently performed with on-the-job training. This implies that colleges have other functions that are not commonly acknowledged. For example, one vital latent function of colleges is to occupy student energy as these individuals wait for entry into the work force. If there weren't so many people enrolled in college, unemployment rates would be much higher and as a consequence crime rates might increase as well. In this light, colleges may occupy the same type of latent function as high schools and elementary schools: daycare.

Sometimes the study of latent functions leads to very surprising conclusions. For example, crime and deviance are commonly believed to undermine social order, and on a manifest level most people perceive no positive consequences of this apparently problematic behavior. Common sense informs us that crime is bad for society and societies would benefit by its eradication. However, all societies display crime and deviance in one form or another. Following functionalist logic, if crime and deviance exist in all societies, they must exist for a reason vital to societal well-being.

On one level, it is certainly harmful (or sometimes fatal) to be on the receiving end of a crime. However, for the society as a whole, crimes sometimes provide a means of connecting people with one another. Consider, for instance, the watercooler discussions that surrounded the O. J. Simpson trial and the speculation concerning the death of JonBenet Ramsey. In each of these circumstances, individuals wholly detached from the crimes were able to use them as a means of generating conversation and thereby connecting with one another. Functionalist theory implies that a reasonable level of crime and deviance may actually be vital to maintaining social order because it increases social cohesion (Erikson 1966).

According to two of the leading experts on sports in society, James Frey and Stanley Eitzen (1991), sports approximate the role of religion in society, particularly in terms of the latent function both institutions have in creating social cohesion. **Social cohesion** refers to the connections that bind people to one another. One of the most important insights of functionalists has been the identification of the mechanisms by which social cohesion is generated and recharged. Interestingly, these mechanisms are strikingly similar in religious ceremonies and sports events.

The manifest function of religion is that it enables individuals to worship a god and to learn about spiritual issues. However, according to Emile Durkheim's (1915/1957) classic study *The Elementary Forms of the Religious Life,* this manifest function disguises a more important latent function, the creation of social cohesion:

> There can be no society which does not feel the need of upholding and reaffirming at regular intervals the collective sentiments and the collective ideas which make its unity and its personality. Now this moral remaking cannot be achieved except by the means of reunions, assemblies and meetings where the individuals, being closely united to one another, reaffirm their common sentiments.... (Durkheim 1957 [1915]; 427)

From Durkheim's perspective, what a religious ceremony is really about, at least in terms of the function for society, is the creation of a feeling of group unity, connectedness, and social cohesion. In order for people to feel spiritually connected with one another, they need to collectively gather and engage in behavior that reaffirms their common bonds to each other.

Durkheim suggested that, left unchecked, social cohesion would naturally diminish over time. The religious ceremony provides an occasion for people to bond with each other and to reaffirm that they are all members of a society that shares common values and beliefs. Metaphorically, the function of a religious ceremony is much like the purpose of an automobile alternator: it is a device to recharge social batteries. By comparing religious ceremonies across different cultures, Durkheim was also able to describe how this recharging mechanism works.

All religions make a distinction between what constitutes the sacred and the profane. The sacred are the deeply held beliefs concerning spirituality and morality. These beliefs are represented in the form of **sacred objects,** tangible items that represent to the group their common values. All religions identify sacred objects. For Christians, these include the cross, the Bible, and holy water. Hindus represent their religion with sacred objects that include statue representations of gods such as Shiva and Krishna. Central to Jewish religion are the Star of David and the Torah. Sacred objects are distinguishable from ordinary things because the group collectively agrees that sacred objects must be treated with great respect. A Christian, for instance, would be deeply offended to witness a Bible being thrown into a recycle bin, even if this is an ecologically sound way to dispose of a book. There is nothing that distinguishes a sacred object from a profane object except for the shared agreement that objects represent what the culture maintains is holy.

All religions also require that members periodically congregate and recognize these sacred objects through rituals. **Rituals** are regularly repeated activities that serve no other purpose outside of the actions themselves. There is no end purpose to a ritual, it is simply done for the sake of doing it.

Rituals direct attention toward sacred objects, and as a consequence focus the group members on the values central to their group's belief systems. It is not accidental, for instance, that the cross is the focal point in a church, or that Native Americans gather in a circular fashion around the totem pole. By collectively gathering in the presence of sacred objects, and by signifying the importance of the sacred objects to the group, religious ceremonies recharge cohesion by forcing people to signify the common bonds that connect one person with one another.

Sports also generate social cohesion and this process is remarkably similar to the methods religions use to make people connect with one another (Lever 1983; Wilkerson and Doddler 1987). Sports events can be characterized as **secular rituals,** in that they are events that adhere to the same principles as religions with the exception of not being linked to otherworldly affairs (Gusfield and Michalowicz 1984). In fact, according to Durkheim, games (sports included) and music, in their earliest forms, were integral parts of religious ceremonies.

Using Durkheim's distinction of the sacred and the profane, the ritualistic aspects of college sports events can be revealed. For example, school colors, pennants signifying past victories, and the school mascot offer symbolic representations of school tradition. The sports team itself also constitutes a sacred object, signifying not only a collection of skilled athletes, but also the university itself. All of these sacred objects provide a means of representing to fans a common identity and signify to members of the university that they are all linked together through collective membership and share common beliefs. When fans shout "Let's Go Notre Dame!" or "Lets Go Orangemen!" they are not just referring to the athletes, they are referring to their university and are linking themselves with the athletes and other fans to form a collective identity.

Moreover, the real excitement of a sporting event is generated not simply by the actions of the team. If this were the case, it would be sufficient to simply watch the game on television, which offers the obvious advantages of instant replays, expert commentary, and comfortable seats, not to mention concerns of ticket prices and parking problems. But as any true fan knows, there is little comparison between watching a televised sporting event and seeing that event in person, just like there is little comparison between watching a televangelist and personally attending a church service. There is a sense of excitement, generated not so much by the athletes but by participating in the ritualistic actions with other fans. The collective singing of fight songs, cheering, and stomping feet all signify to the members present that they are part of a common group. Interestingly, so deep is this sense of connection that the spontaneous chants that emerge at games (such as "loser, loser, loser") are instantaneously tonally harmonious (Heaton 1992), much like chants in religious ceremonies.

Sports and the Creation of Group Boundaries

Functionalists also highlight the need for groups to establish unique identities. Once an identity is created, it enables members of the group to develop a shared sense of belonging. Sports contribute to this aspect of social relationships by facilitating the creation of **in groups** and **out groups.** Wearing school colors or logos is a means by which members of college society demonstrate their membership in the in group, as does attendance at the sporting events. The **out group** constitutes those people who do not meet membership criteria (Sherif et al. 1988), and at college athletic events, the in group/out group status is clearly marked. For instance, at college games opponent teams are commonly disparaged, signifying that this group is inferior and separate from one's own team. Fans do this by feigning boredom when opponents are introduced (such as holding up newspapers), or by yelling disparaging things about the opposing team. At a recent Cornell hockey game, when the announcer said "And now the starting lineup for Clarkson," the fans responded in unison "Is that a real school?" At this same game, fans of the Clarkson team were seated in the visitors' section and were periodically greeted with taunts of "Section O Sucks!" Thus the ritualistic elements of an intercollegiate competition also help people construct these in group and out group divisions, further heightening their abilities to create connections with one another.

Summary of Sports and Social Cohesion

Functionalists are inclined to view the social world as operating on the basis of equilibrium, with different social institutions functioning to create and maintain social harmony. This perspective leads analysts to interpret sports as reflecting and reinforcing deep underlying cultural values that maintain social order. It also reveals that sports provide a safety-valve function, releasing tension stemming from cultural contradictions. The functionalist perspective also reveals that sports operate much like religions, creating a sense of social cohesion through sacred objects and ritualistic encounters.

While sports may promote physical well-being, generate some revenue for universities, and offer some entertainment value, their more important latent function is to create and reinforce a sense of college spirit. Without sports, colleges would more likely be defined simply as places where people study, take exams, and attend classes. Sports provide a means of shaping a collective identity and defining colleges as places where members are connected with each other on a deeper, more spiritual level. It is not incidental that attendance at a sports event is a way of demonstrating one's "college spirit."

Although the functionalist perspective opens up many insights on the positive role sports play in college and society, it does have limitations. Conflict theorists, critical of the functionalist perspective, argue that these limitations can be revealed by reorienting the sociological imagination away from the notion of the world as being based on order. What happens if the foundations of society are reconceptualized as not being based upon social harmony, but rather on competition and conflict over limited resources?

Sports and Social Conflict

Can it be assumed that, just because a society is functioning, this society serves the interests of all groups in an equitable manner? Unlike functionalists, who tend to answer this question in the affirmative, conflict theorists approach this question with a considerable degree of skepticism. Conflict theorists place the question of fairness in existing social relations as paramount in their examination in social relations, conceiving society as an arena where competitions for limited resources are played out. As functionalist theory draws upon the work of Emile Durkheim, the conflict perspective draws heavily upon the work of Karl Marx, who wrote in the *Communist Manifesto* that "the history of all hitherto existing societies, is a history of class conflict" (1848/1972).

The conflict perspective reorients the analysis of society as the study of struggles between people as they compete for control over limited resources. Conflict theorists begin with the assumption that society is a place where some people, by virtue of their class position or status, are able to gather disproportionate shares of wealth and power. It is also a place where other people, by virtue of being members of minority groups or the lower class, are exploited to serve the interests of the more privileged.

Central to conflict theory is the role social inequality plays in shaping the structure of society. The operations of government, religion, and even sports, are intricately linked with issues of poverty, exploitation, wealth, and privilege in society. Before discussing how sports fit into this larger picture of inequality, it will be helpful to highlight just a few indicators that reveal the degree of social inequality present in the United States. Surprisingly, many Americans are ignorant of the degree of social inequality present in their own society. As I will suggest below, sports may actually play a role in establishing this ignorance.

One way to measure social inequality is to compare the disparity in incomes received by different social groups. For example, in the United States, the richest fifth of the population receives nearly half of the total income earned in a given year. In comparison, the poorest fifth of the population receives only 5 percent of the total income earned (Gilbert and Kahl 1993). Comparisons of wealth, the total assets that an individual or family possesses, reveal an even more dramatic disparity between the richest and poorest members of society. In 1990, the richest 10 percent of households controlled over two thirds (69%) of the wealth in the United States and possessed nearly all of the stocks (84%) and bonds (94%). In contrast, nearly half of the adult population (44%) can be considered nearly propertyless, owning total net assets of less than $25,000 (Gilbert and Kahl 1993).

There are also important demographic differences between the affluent and the disadvantaged members of society. The chances of being poor are strongly related to ethnicity. White Americans stand a one-in-ten chance of being poor. In contrast nearly one in three blacks lives below the poverty line, and more than one in four Hispanics live below the poverty line. Poverty is also strongly related to gender and family structure, as evidenced by nearly half of minority female-headed families living below the poverty line (Gilbert and Kahl 1993). Likewise, comparably few women or minorities achieve high levels of power and privilege. For example, in 1994, only 7 percent of chief executive officers at Fortune 1000 companies were female and only 3 percent were black (Zweigenhaft and Domhoff 1998).

Reproducing Class and Ethnic Inequality in College Sports

College athletics are intricately linked with economic concerns. Universities expend large amounts of money on building and maintaining stadiums, as well as recruiting and training star athletes. The University of Michigan, for instance, spent $5,400,000 just on athletic scholarships during the 1992–1993 academic year (Sack and Staurowski 1998). Collectively, Division I universities annually award over $500 million in athletic scholarships (Naughton 1997). Universities that participate in the NCAA Division I men's basketball tournament make roughly $35 million and college football bowl games generate over $30 million for the competing teams (Sage 1990). Clearly, college athletics is big business.

Although the majority of schools do not make money from intercollegiate sports (Salter 1996), the University of Connecticut offers a poignant example of what a successful intercollegiate athletic program can do for a university. According to its president, Philip E. Austin, the support of athletics has helped the university recruit students, enhanced its ability to garner funding from the state legislature, and energized alumni to give philanthropic support. The data bears out his argument. From 1994 to 1999, as the University of Connecticut put increasing support into athletics, campus tours of prospective students have risen from 9000 to 12,000 students. University donations increased from $6 million to $20 million per year. Immediately following the Huskies' victory in the NCAA basketball finals, the university secured $1 billion from the Connecticut state legislature (Allen 1999).

College athletics can be a means for students to obtain scholarships and gain entry into professional sports, as well as provide an avenue out of the ghetto or the small farming town. The former University of Kentucky quarterback, Tim Couch, knows firsthand the rewards sports can bring after receiving a record $48 million contract, as well as a $12.2 million signing bonus with the Cleveland Browns (Freeman 1999). Given the huge financial incentives professional sports offer, it is understandable why many high school students strive for coveted positions on a Division I team and hope for future careers in professional sports.

On the surface, college athletics and intercollegiate sports seem to be a win-win proposition for colleges and students, but it is important to recognize that for every dream fulfilled, hundreds are deferred. According to Sage (1990) the likelihood of a male high school athlete becoming a professional is about 1 in 10,000. The chances for female athletes are even smaller, in part because there are fewer women's professional sports. The odds for black male athletes are somewhat better (1 in 3500), but are still dauntingly low. While sports are commonly perceived to be a pathway to success, particularly among the lower-class and ethnic minorities, statistics such as these indicate that the likelihood of even a skilled high school or college student "making it" in the world of professional athletics is slim. Of course, many students strive for careers that are highly competitive and not all will achieve their goals of becoming lawyers, doctors, or professional basketball players. However, unlike the curriculum designed to train students for more conventional careers, the curriculum designed for college athletes in top schools is often so narrowly focused that it offers little preparation for careers outside professional athletics.

As the financial stakes for successful college athletic teams increase, so does the inclination to recruit students solely for their abilities on the field. For example, a study by economist Roger Noll revealed that the departure of quarterback John Paye resulted in a net decline of $400,000 in revenues for Stanford University (Shropshire 1990). Not only does money come through ticket admissions and broadcast contracts, it also comes through corporate contracts. For example, Nike has sponsorship agreements with eleven colleges, including Florida State, Penn State, and the University of Alabama. In 1995, McDonald's offered Georgia Tech $5.5 million to display its corporate logo inside and outside of its basketball arena (Sack and Staurowski 1998). In the words of two critics of college athletic programs:

> At Notre Dame, an athletic scholarship is worth about $25,000 per year. Although this seems like a princely sum to parents struggling to pay a child's educational expenses, it cannot compare to the financial benefits derived by other major stakeholders in the college sport industry. (Sack and Staurowski 1998; 93)

Even though college athletes work long hours and generate considerable sums of money both for the entertainment industry and their universities, courts have consistently held that college athletes are not employees working under labor contracts (*Colemen* v. *Western Michigan University* 1983, *Rensing* v. *Indiana State University Board* 1983; Sage 1990). In contrast, college coaches commonly earn salaries in excess of $100,000. Compensation from corporations, such as Nike, can effectively double their base income (Shropshire 1990).

According to Guttman (1988), student athletes are commonly recruited and admitted to colleges even when they lack the academic background to succeed in higher education. For instance, in 1984, basketball player Chris Washburn was recruited by 150 universities, even though he was unable to answer a single question correctly on his verbal SAT. Occasional reports reveal the extent to which student athletes are unprepared to perform even the most rudimentary college level work. As one sad example, consider the following portion of an essay submitted by a college athlete at the University of Southern California in an upper-division speech communication course:

> I when went John because He had a point on girl that I couldn't not again, so that made me think girl don't have body for lady unless they wont that why I went with John. (Quoted in Guttman 1988; 113)

The NCAA currently supports a policy of minimal attainment on the SAT, but all too often there is little similarity between the academic potential of students admitted on athletic scholarships and their classmates. Upon entry into college, assistant coaches counsel their students to take "gut" courses that will keep them eligible for competition. Marginally prepared athletes are advised to register for courses with appropriate nicknames such as "rocks for jocks" or "clap for credit." This advice is understandable, considering that competitive intercollegiate sports commonly require a commitment of 40 to 60 hours per week from student athletes. The average major college football player works 2200 hours per year, about 55 hours per week, and basketball players devote about 50 hours per week during their seasons (Sage 1990). With schedules such as these, clearly academic courses are the extracurricular activity for student athletes, not sports.

One particularly egregious example of the priority colleges place on athletes' academic accomplishment is offered by the University of Minnesota basketball team in the 1990s, as documented in a Pulitzer Prize-winning series of articles by George Dohrmann. From 1994 to 1998, at least 20 men's basketball players at the University of Minnesota had research papers, take-home exams, or coursework done for them by a staff counselor. The team's academic counseling was set up to be independent of the academic counseling center, and as a consequence its activities received little supervision. In addition to academic fraud, the reports also document last-minute grade changes and advising of athletes to take inappropriate courses—actions that were intended to keep players eligible for competition. After intense public scrutiny, the president of the University of Minnesota eventually announced the termination of the head coach's tenure at the school stating that "numerous, and maybe even massive incidents of academic misconduct" occurred involving the men's basketball team (Dohrmann et al. 1999a).

Given the marginal preparedness of many athletes for college work, and given the heavy workload college athletics places on students, it isn't surprising that student athletes do not perform at levels comparable with academically oriented students (Naughton 1997). One report estimated that 80% of black NCAA Division I football and basketball players never graduate from their universities (Lapchick 1988). Another report, based on data compiled by the NCAA, revealed that many of the top college basketball teams (including University of Cincinnati, University of Michigan, Syracuse University, and Gonzaga University), failed to graduate a single black basketball player within six years of their initial enrollment between 1989 and 1992 (Peoples 2000).

There may be a temptation to find fault in those student athletes who fail to achieve their athletic aspirations or fulfill academic requirements for success in other fields. Framed according to individualistic thinking, this may make sense, but sociologically, it constitutes **blaming the victim** (Sage 1990). To blame the victim is to place the responsibility of a social problem on the people who are at the receiving end of that problem (Valentine 1968). Some student athletes perceive athletics as a ticket out of a life of unemployment and dead-end jobs. Their aspirations for an unconventional career path are shaped by experiencing life in families that have had little success, and by living in communities with poor schools and high unemployment rates. Lacking requisite academic skills when recruited for college, and burdened with an intense practice schedule, student athletes sacrifice classes for the game. When these students fail to be recruited for a professional sport, or simply fail out of college, they are replaced with another up-and-coming high school senior. The process repeats itself, keeping intact a system of exploitation for another class of student athletes. Charles Farrell, director of Rainbow Sports, a division of the Rainbow/PUSH Wall Street Project, summarizes the situation of college basketball teams as "sinister" and concludes:

> Those schools, especially Cincinnati, had about two kids go pro. They are not all playing pro basketball. That's a cop out. They are taking black kids, and using them and spitting them out at the other end. (Peoples 2000; 45)

Intercollegiate sports also reflect the tendency in society to relegate ethnic minorities to subsidiary positions and exclude them from positions of power. One common way ethnic inequality is reproduced in athletics is through a process known as **stacking.** Stacking involves the disproportionate allotment of minorities into subsidiary positions and whites into positions that offer opportunities to exercise authority and responsibility. Coaches have historically placed white players in commanding positions such as football quarterback, baseball pitcher, hockey goalie, and volleyball setter (Eitzen and Furst 1989; Lapchick 1988; Lavoie 1989; Leonard 1987). The process of stacking is also evident in management of athletic teams. According to Sage (1990), in 1989, only five major university football teams and only ten basketball teams were coached by African Americans, and almost all black coaches were employed as assistants. Stacking reinforces inequality as minority athletes forgo financial rewards associated with the central positions on teams. It also casts members of minority groups into positions that require minimal intellectual skills and reinforces stereotypes that equate minority status with brutishness or lower intelligence (Guttman 1988; Hoberman 1997).

Reproducing Gender Inequality in College Sports

It is interesting to observe that most sports in college society (and in the wider society) are strictly sex segregated. For sports like football, hockey, and gymnastics, the need for sex segregation is commonly attributed to innate biological differences. On the other hand, sex segregation also exists in sports that are not reliant on body size or strength, such as marksmanship, billiards, and curling. Some feminist analysts have suggested that dividing sports into male teams and female teams serves to **reify** the differences between men and women (Festle 1996; Nelson 1991). To reify is to make ideas or beliefs real by acting on these beliefs. In sports the physical inferiority of women is created in part through a belief that women are not capable of performing at a level comparable to men. For example, in comparison with the criteria for boys, the criteria for the President's Physical Fitness Award for girls requires five fewer sit-ups, three fewer pull-ups, and allows nearly a minute and a half extra time for a mile run. Possibly the very act of expecting less of girls increases the likelihood that girls will internalize beliefs that they cannot perform at the same level as boys. Nelson (1991) offers compelling data that suggest that American society underestimates female competitiveness in the world of sports, and that sports do not necessarily have to be sex segregated. For instance, Janet Evans' world record freestyle swims in 1988 in the 800-meter and 1500-meter would have been world-record times for men in 1972. Susan Butcher's four wins in the grueling Iditarod dogsled race also offer compelling evidence that women can compete simply as athletes and not as "female athletes."

Interviews with women athletes indicate that they are subtly and not so subtly pressured not to engage in sports or to direct their energies to sports, such as gymnastics and figure skating, that coincide with traditional feminine characteristics (Festle 1996; Nelson 1991). It is interesting to observe that men are largely absent from female-oriented sports, but women play integral roles in supporting men's sports. Cheerleading positions, for instance, cast women as support personnel and reaffirm cultural understandings of women as sex objects. Imagine a gender inversion, with men in skimpy outfits jumping and cheering for a women's basketball team. The degree to which this is inconceivable reveals cultural expectations of men's and women's responsibilities toward each other in the world of sports, and to some extent in the wider society. The relegation of cheerleading to women also serves to reaffirm the salience of sexuality as a defining concern for women. In contrast, ethnographic studies reveal that men involved in contact sports adopt heightened masculine values. In this way sports increase the divide between males and females in society (Foley 1990; Guttman 1988).

Women athletes also face hurdles in gaining recognition, support, and mentoring in athletics. Women are grossly underrepresented in the ranks of sports journalists, photographers, and publishers, comprising only 9 percent of the people employed in these positions (Nelson 1991). Women are also underrepresented in the administration of athletic teams. Nearly all (99%) of the coaches servicing college men are male, but in contrast, only half of the coaches servicing college women are female (Salter 1996). In 1996, there were only six female athletic directors at NCAA Division I schools, leading one analyst to conclude that women have a better chance of becoming the president of one of these universities than heading the athletic department (Salter 1996). In the late 1980s, male students received approximately three-fourths of the money spent on recruiting student athletes and male athletes received $180 million more in scholarships than female college athletes. Also, the vast majority of athletic departments' operating budgets (77%) were devoted to male sports (NCAA 1990). In a society that tends to devalue women's accomplishments, it is not surprising that male-oriented college sports continue to receive considerably more financial support and public attention than female-oriented sports (Nelson 1991).

At the Fort Collins campus in Colorado in 1972, the women's athletic program received $5500, a paltry sum compared with the men's athletic program, which received $1.4 million (Salter 1996). That same year, Congress passed Title IX, which ostensibly forbade sexual discrimination in schools that receive federal funding. The law was intended to insure that female students receive comparable educational support to male students, and courts later interpreted this to include equitable support of women's athletic programs. Before Title IX, fewer than 15% of college athletes were women (Sage 1990), but by the early 1990s this figure had risen to 34% (Nelson 1991). In the wake of Title IX, there have been considerable advances in funding and generating participation in women's sports, but women still face considerable barriers as athletes and much progress is still needed.

Sports and Hegemony

Early conflict theorists, Marx included, believed that the increasingly obvious disparities in wealth between the owners of industry (*the bourgeoisie*) and the working class (*the proletariat*) would spur the working class to revolt.

When Marx concluded the *Communist Manifesto* (1848/1972) with the phrase "Working men of the world unite!", it seemed only a matter of time until the revolution would take place. Even though the Marxist vision of a classless society has largely been discredited both through social theory and through historical example, the conflict perspective continues to offer interesting questions and answers about the workings of capitalist societies like the United States. One of the most important questions concerns why the disenfranchised members of this society are not rising up and rebelling.

Recall that the functionalist perspective suggests that religion and sports contribute to the operations of the entire social system through their ability to generate social cohesion. On the other hand, conflict theorists are inclined to point to the tranquilizing effects both institutions have on political activism. In a society rife with inequality and exploitation, sports and religion sometimes serve to distract people from social problems and focus their time and energy on pleasant, but inconsequential, diversions. Karl Marx identified this aspect of religion in the *Communist Manifesto* (1848/1972), labeling it "the opiate of the masses." Believing that religion has effects comparable to narcotics, Marx suggested that it sedated the disenfranchised and kept them from rebelling for equality.

According to Antonio Gramsci (1932/1991), members of the upper class are likely to develop belief systems, or **ideologies,** that reaffirm the legitimacy of their privileged positions. If the lower classes adopt these same ideologies, they will be inclined to believe that the existing social system operates in their interests as well. When the lower classes believe that existing social institutions are serving their interests in the same way as they are serving the upper classes, they tend to resist political actions that could potentially reshape society towards greater equality between the classes. In this way, the upper classes gain power through **hegemony,** the pervasive intrusion of their own understandings of reality throughout all of society. The power of hegemony stems from beliefs that the current social structure is either inevitable or desirable, when neither is necessarily true.

Religion can play a considerable role in creating hegemony and instilling upper class ideologies in the lower classes. In the study *Millhands and Preachers* (1942/1958), for example, Liston Pope examined the role churches played in labor union movements in the early twentieth century. Pope studied the response of church leaders to union activists, who were attempting to organize workers in a factory town. Like other cotton-mill workers, in 1929 the workers in Gastonia, North Carolina, labored long hours for little pay in hazardous working conditions. Pope found that in the period before, during, and after an intense labor strike, none of the church services in the town addressed the social and political crisis facing the community. Instead, the church services for poor members of the community were filled with dancing, singing, and clapping. These services offered little more than a distraction from hardship.

Ministers in churches that serviced the mill employees preached the rewards that hard work and faithfulness would produce in the afterlife. By emphasizing "pie in the sky" theology, these ministers helped instill values that implicitly discouraged political activism among their congregation. The services in the mill owners' churches were primarily concerned with abstract theological questions such as the meaning of faith. In none of the services were the moral issues relating to the strike, unionization, wages, armed violence, or worker safety ever raised.

Hegemony was created because the ministers worked either directly or indirectly for the mills and received their paychecks at the mill payroll offices. By employing ministers who shared their own ways of understanding the world, mill owners were able to disseminate their own belief systems through the churches and prevent alternate ideas from entering the community. One way they did this was by using ministers to screen potential employees for "moral integrity." While performing this task, ministers inquired into applicants' marital status, use of alcohol, and attitudes toward unions. Those applicants that the ministers deemed morally suspect (i.e., single men, drinkers, or union sympathizers) were not offered jobs. In that residence in Gastonia was largely dependent on having a job in a cotton mill, the mill owners were able to limit the types of ideas discussed inside and outside of their factory walls. As a consequence of the collusion between mill owners and preachers, a considerable proportion of the members of the Gastonia community were resistant to the efforts of union activists, believing that unionization ran counter to national, community, and company interests.

Conflict theory suggests that people share common concerns by virtue of their class position, gender, or minority status. When they unite and develop a sense of **class consciousness,** they stand the greatest chance of improving their life chances. Some analyses suggest that sports undermine class, gender, and ethnic unity (e.g., Hargreaves 1986; Sage 1990). One way sports do this is by cultivating loyalties away from class identities. As means of illustration, consider the role that company baseball teams had on working-class unity. Through much of the twentieth century, it was common for industries in small towns to sponsor company baseball teams. These teams would compete against other company teams in other communities. So serious was the competition that some workers, just like some college students, would be employed for no reason other than they were good at bat.

According to June Nash (1989) these company teams offered managers a context where they were able to generate worker loyalty to the corporation. It provided a venue in which workers and management could congregate in order to cheer the company team against rival teams from neighboring communities. By fostering worker identification with the factory, managers were then able to use this as a means of creating a sense of shared interests that spanned class lines to include workers, managers, and owners. Once this definition of the situation was created, it became possible to convince workers to forego raises or improvements in working conditions because all were sharing in the fight to keep the company "competitive." The teams also created rivalries and severed worker loyalties to other workers laboring in different communities or for other companies. Thus while one form of unity was created through the sport, politically charged forms of unity were undermined. Nash suggests that company baseball teams were part of a wider program that dissuaded workers from thinking of their position in class terms and created worker allegiance toward corporate interests.

A sense of national identity is also commonly created through sports events (Prisuta 1979), and this sometimes works to the detriment of disenfranchised groups (Wenner 1989). This process is especially important in understanding the role sports play in underdeveloped nations, as summarized by James Frey (1988):

> Sport enables society to cohere by linking diverse groups in a common frame of reference in which symbols share common meaning, transcending political and social barriers. The elite and the masses are brought together in a sports arena and status differences are neutralized and a semblance of democracy is established.... Potential internal conflicts are avoided or neutralized by transferring the hostility and aggression from the street to the arena. (Frey 1988; 68)

This observation can be illustrated by examining the ideals versus the realities of competitions such as the Olympic Games. The ideals forwarded by the International Olympic Committee are for the Olympics to create mutual respect among young people through sport and to promote international friendship and cooperation between nations. Critics of the Olympic movement, however, question the degree to which the games actually accomplish these goals. Although the games require some degree of cooperation, the events are competitive and in the end provide a demonstration of the superiority (and inferiority) of participating nations (Heinila 1985). Olympic competitions are wholly unbalanced, with Third World nations standing little chance of garnering a proportionate share of Olympic medals. The success of First World nations can be largely attributed to the wealth these nations have to invest in facilities, training, health care, nutrition, and all of the other things that will create superstar athletes (Espy 1979). As the First World nations accumulate medals, the Olympics reinforce ideologies that proclaim the superiority of the First World, and the cultural inferiority of the Third World.

The power of hegemony can also be observed in events such as football games, which instill values that are sympathetic to the actions of the upper classes. As one cultural critic suggested about the Super Bowl:

> The structural values of the Super Bowl can be summarized succinctly: North American professional football is an aggressive, strictly regulated team game

fought between males who use both violence and technology to gain control of property for the economic gain of individuals within a nationalistic entertainment context. The Super Bowl propagates these values by elevating one game to the level of a spectacle of American ideology collectively celebrated. (Real 1975; 42)

Competitive sports offer lessons concerning what constitutes socially appropriate conduct. Vince Lombardi's maxim, "winning isn't everything, it's the only thing," guides both athletic competitions and economic transactions. When members of a society agree on a cultural value such as this, it becomes acceptable for corporations to pay poverty level wages, to lay off employees at will, and to deliberately structure work policies that limit accessibility to health insurance. In the world of college athletics, these lessons are taught again and again, as society is modeled on the playing field.

Summary of Sports and Social Conflict

The conflict perspective highlights the ways in which sports fit into a larger program of exploitation, discrimination, and inequality in society. In many ways, sports exemplify tendencies in society to exploit workers, particularly workers from lower socioeconomic groups and ethnic minorities, for profit motives. The conflict perspective also reveals how the power of the upper classes is enhanced through the cultural embrace of competitive sports. Sports have the power to dilute and fragment subordinate members of society into small competing factions. As sports divert people from forming a collective identity, it undermines their ability to position themselves to work together to enact political change. Also, sports instill the ideologies that are sympathetic to the interests of the upper class. By teaching disenfranchised groups to understand the world in the same way that privileged groups understand the world, sports provide a means of legitimating inequality in society (Hargreaves 1986).

Discussion

Anthropological analysis of sports highlights the central role sports play in society, reflecting prevailing norms and values within the society. The functionalist and conflict perspectives offer contrasting visions of the impact sports have on colleges and society. From the functionalist perspective, sports are akin to religion, providing rituals and sacred objects that reinforce a collective identity and shared sense of belonging. While much of college life revolves around academics, without intercollegiate athletics, the sense of commitment to universities would probably weaken. At the same time, the conflict perspective highlights some aspects of intercollegiate athletics that are open to criticism and directs attention toward aspects of sports on campus that need considerable improvement.

Wall Street and college administrators have discovered that sometimes the passion from athletic events can be milked for financial gain. It appears that, as financial rewards for the production of a winning college team increase, so do the incentives for placing the academic needs of college athletes secondary to their athletic performance. Evidence of this trend includes the recruitment of student athletes who are unlikely to achieve academic success even under the most favorable conditions, as well as construction of training schedules that distract student athletes from their coursework. As profit motives enter intercollegiate athletics, colleges are developing the same types of exploitive practices that occur in the wider society.

Some have suggested that student athletes should be treated more as employees than as students, and that they should receive compensation in accordance with their financial contributions to college society (Sack and Staurowsky 1998). This solution requires a conceptual shift, thinking of the needs of athlete students, as opposed to student athletes. It also opens a variety of questions relating to the degree to which these athletes should be compensated, as well as reevaluating the academic expectations for athlete students. For example, if the athletes are employees of the college, need they take any courses? If they are employees, will sports still serve to unite the campus community?

An alternate approach is to consider ways of prioritizing the student component of the student athlete role to insure that all student athletes have the opportunity to graduate with a meaningful academic degree. At the institutional level, this could involve individual colleges reflecting on strategies, programs, and policies that enable athletes to balance the rigors of their sporting activities with their needs for academic success. At a larger level, this may also require instituting more dependable mechanisms to enforce agreements with colleges and universities to maintain minimal academic standards for recruitment and retention of student athletes.

It is also important to recognize that the problem of academic incompetence among some student athletes comes from inadequate schooling at the high school and even elementary levels. No matter how motivated student athletes are, without a decent educational foundation, the likelihood of their success in college will be modest. At an even more basic level, the motivations to pursue athletics as a career can come in part from living in low-income communities where conventional career opportunities appear blocked (see MacLeod 1995). Ameliorating this concern requires rethinking about how poor families are integrated into the larger social structure and about the factors that create poverty in the first place.

Another question for the college community concerns the ways in which intercollegiate sports shape social values. Both the functionalist and conflict theories affirm that college sports reflect and reinforce the behaviors and values propagated in the wider society. Competitive sports reward people who work their hardest to win, and in this way help create workers who will try their best to tackle difficult problems with persistence and creativity. At the same time, competitive sports also cultivate attitudes that support a "win at any cost" mentality. In this way competitive sports play a role in socializing people to do nearly anything to come out on top, even when that involves structuring relationships that are detrimental to other individuals or the wider social order.

This mind-set has caused a variety of social problems. The late twentieth century, for instance, saw the closure of hundreds of factories in the United States, not because these factories were unprofitable, but because they were not profitable enough. It also saw a small group of corporate raiders loot the assets of and bankrupt healthy companies in order to create quick profits for small groups of investors (Barlett and Steele 1992). Few would argue that these types of behaviors are desirable, yet sports indirectly contribute to these practices by modeling these behaviors on the playing field. One of the challenges facing colleges in the twenty-first century is educating people to be competitive *and* sensitive to broader social concerns. Possibly college athletics can aid this endeavor by offering lessons that enable us to rethink what it means to win. One way colleges are currently working in this direction is by offering courses involving "new games." These games involve group cooperation to solve difficult or challenging problems, without creating a winning or a losing team, and thus minimize the antagonism that develops in competitive circumstances (see Sherif et al. 1988).

Gender equity also remains a concern for colleges, universities, and the wider society. Even though Title IX has produced considerable advances for women in sports, there is much room for improvement. There are two overarching concerns suggested in the above analysis. The first issue is the degree to which women's sports are supported compared with men's sports. As long as universities give women's teams less financial support, women will likely lag behind men in their athletic accomplishments. Colleges can also use intercollegiate athletics as a means of offering symbolic support to women students as well. For instance, homecoming events can be structured around a women's team as opposed to a men's team, and college newspapers could feature female student athletes' accomplishments as prominently as those of male athletes.

Another concern is the continued sex segregation of athletic events. So long as women and men are cast into a gender apartheid, it is unlikely that their accomplishments will reach parity. Solutions to the gender segregation issues may require "thinking outside of the box." For example, one solution could be to divide teams according to weight and skill level, as opposed to gender (Nelson 1991). Actually, these practices are already being done within sex-segregated sports, such as wrestling and boxing (divisions based on weight) and basketball and football (varsity versus junior varsity teams). This approach effectively accommodates biological differences, puts men and women on an even playing field, and minimizes the distinction between student status as male or female.

The contrasting visions of the functionalist and conflict perspectives leads to a complex understanding of the role of sports in college and society. The functionalist perspective highlights the ways that sports integrate people in society and maintain some level of social harmony. On the other hand, the conflict perspective reveals discrepancies between groups in society, leading to concerns of how sports reflect and contribute to inequitable social relationships. The challenge of creating a society in which all groups experience fair opportunities is considerable. The degree to which we have the power to identify and respond to these concerns, on and off the playing field, rests on our ability think seriously about the foundations of social relationships.

REFERENCES

Allen, Mike. 1999. "UConn Finds Rich Off-Court Gains in Basketball." *New York Times* May 31, B1–2.

Barlett, Donald and James Steele. 1992. *America: What Went Wrong?* Kansas City: Andrews and McMeel.

Bellah, Robert, Richard Madsen, William Sullivan, Ann Swidler, and Steven Tipton. 1985. *Habits of the Heart: Individualism and Commitment in American Life.* New York: Harper and Row.

Berliner, David and Bruce Biddle. 1995. *The Manufactured Crisis: Myths, Fraud, and the Attack on America's Public Schools.* Reading, MA: Addison-Wesley.

Bilger, Burkhard. 1999. "Enter the Chicken." *Harpers.* March 1999. 298:48–57.

Cady, Edwin. 1978. *The Big Game: College Sports and American Life.* Knoxville: University of Tennessee Press.

Chandler, Alfred. 1990. *Scale and Scope: The Dynamics of Industrial Capitalism.* Cambridge: Belknap Press.

Colemen v. Western Michigan University. 1983. 336 N.W. 2d. 224.

Dohrmann, George, Judith Yates Borger, Rick Linsk, Blake Morrison, Debra O'Connor, Kristian Pope, Paul Totso, and Larry Millett. 1999. "'A 1.5 Million Goodby://'Mutual Break with U. Carries No Reprimand." *St. Paul Pioneer Press.* June 26, 1A.

Durkheim, Emile. 1957 [1915]. *The Elementary Forms of the Religious Life.* London: Allen and Unwin.

Eitzen, D. Stanley and David Furst. 1989. "Racial Bias in Women's Collegiate Volleyball." *Journal of Sport and Social Issues.* 13:46–51.

Erikson, Kai. 1966. *Wayward Puritans: A Study in the Sociology of Deviance.* New York: Wiley.

Espy, Richard. 1979. *The Politics of the Olympic Games.* Los Angeles: University of California Press.

Festle, Mary Jo. 1996. *Playing Nice: Politics and Apologies in Women's Sports.* New York: Columbia University Press.

Foley, Douglas. 1990. "The Great American Football Ritual: Reproducing Race, Class, and Gender Inequality." *Sociology of Sport Journal.* 7:111–135.

Freeman, Mike. 1999. "Picking Quarterbacks as Easy as 1-2-3." *New York Times* April 18 8:1–2.

Frey, James. 1988. "The Internal and External Role of Sport in National Development." *Journal of National Development*. 1:65–82.

Frey, James and D. Stanley Eitzen. 1991. "Sport and Society." *Annual Review of Sociology*. 17:503–522.

Galbraith, John Kenneth. 1976. *The Affluent Society (3rd Edition)*. Boston: Houghton Mifflin.

Geertz, Clifford. 1973. *The Interpretation of Cultures: Selected Essays*. New York: Basic Books.

Gilbert, Dennis and Joseph Kahl. 1993. *The American Class Structure: A New Synthesis*. Belmont, Calif.: Wadsworth.

Gramsci, Antonio. 1991 [1932]. *Prison Notebooks*. New York: Columbia University Press.

Gray, John. 1992. *Men Are from Mars, Women Are from Venus*. New York: Harper-Collins.

Gusfield, Joseph and Jerzy Michalowicz. 1984. "Secular Symbolism: Studies of Ritual, Ceremony, and the Symbolic Order in Modern Life." *Annual Review of Sociology*. 10:417–435.

Guttman, Allen. 1988. *A Whole New Ball Game: An Interpretation of American Sports*. Chapel Hill: University of North Carolina Press.

Haerle, Rudolf. 1974. "The Athlete as 'Moral' Leader: Heroes, Success Themes and Basic Cultural Values in Selected Baseball Autobiographies, 1900–1970." *Journal of Popular Culture*. 8:392–401.

Hargreaves, John. 1986. *Sport, Power and Culture*. New York: St. Martins Press.

Heaton, C. P. 1992. "Air Ball: Spontaneous Large-Group Precision Chanting." *Popular Music and Society*. 16:81–83.

Heinila, Kalevi. 1985. "Sport and International Understanding—A Contradiction in Terms?" *Sociology of Sport Journal*. 2:240–248.

Hoberman, John. 1997. *Darwin's Athletes: How Sport Has Damaged Black America and Preserved the Myth of Race*. Boston: Houghton Mifflin.

Kozol, Jonathan. 1991. *Savage Inequalities: Children in America's Schools*. New York: Crown Publishing.

Lapchick, R. E. 1988. "Discovering Fool's Gold on the Golden Horizon." *The World and I*. 3:603–611.

Lavoie, Marc. 1989. "Stacking, Performance Differentials, and Salary Discrimination in Professional Ice Hockey: A Survey of the Evidence". *Sociology of Sport Journal*. 6:17–53.

Leonard, Wilbert. 1987. "Stacking in College Basketball: A Neglected Analysis." *Sociology of Sport Journal*. 4:403–409.

MacLeod, Jay. 1995. *Ain't No Makin' It: Leveled Aspirations in a Low-Income Neighborhood*. Boulder: Westview Press.

Marglin, Steven. 1982. "What Do Bosses Do?" in Giddens, Anthony and David Held [eds.], *Classes, Power and Conflict: Classical and Contemporary Debates*. Berkeley: University of California Press.

Marx, Karl and Friedrich Engels. 1972 [1848]. "Manifesto of the Communist Party." in Tucker, Robert C., [ed.], *The Marx-Engels Reader*. New York: W.W. Norton.

Mason, Tony. 1995. *Passion of the People? Football in South America*. New York: Verso.

Mills, C. Wright. 1959. *The Sociological Imagination*. New York: Oxford University Press.

Morgan, Kathleen O'Leary and Scott Morgan. 1997. *State Rankings 1997*. Lawrence KS: Morgan Quitno.

Nash, June. 1989. *From Tank Town to High Tech: The Class of Community and Industrial Cycles*. Albany: State University of New York.

National Collegiate Athletic Association. 1990. *Gender Equity Study*. Overland Park, KS: NCAA.

Naughton, Jim. 1997. "Athletes on Top-Ranked Teams Lack Grades and Test Scores of Other Students." *The Chronicle of Higher Education* 25 July 1997 A43–44.

Naughton, Jim. 1997. "Women in Division 1 Sports Programs: 'The Glass is Half Empty and Half Full'". *The Chronicle of Higher Education* 11 April 1997 A39–40.

Nelson, Mariah Burton. 1991. *Are We Winning Yet? How Women Are Changing Sports and Sports Are Changing Women.* New York: Random House.

New York Times. "A Nike Raise in Indonesia." March 24, 1999. p. 21.

Pearton, Robert. 1986. "Violence in Sport and the Special Case of Soccer Hooliganism in the United Kingdom." in Rees, Roger and Andrew Miracle [eds.], *Sport and Social Theory.* Champaign, IL: Human Kinetics.

Peoples, Betsy. 2000. "Bottom 50." *Emerge.* April, 44–45.

Pope, Lison. 1958 [1942]. *Millhands and Preachers: A Study of Gastonia.* New Haven: Yale University Press.

Powers, Richard. 1992. "Sports and American Culture." in Luedtke, Luther [ed.], *Making America: The Society and Culture of the United States.* Chapel Hill: University of North Carolina Press.

Prisuta, Robert. 1979. "Televised Sport and Political Values." *Journal of Communication.* 29:94–102.

Real, M. R. 1975. "Super Bowl: Mythic Spectacle." *Journal of Communication.* 25:31–43.

Reisman, David and Reuel Denney. 1971. "Football in America: A Study in Cultural Diffusion" in Elias, Norbert [ed.], *The Sociology of Sport.* London: Frank Cass and Company.

Rensing v. Indiana State University Board. 1983. 444 N.E. 2d. 1170.

Rosovsky, Henry. 1990. *The University: An Owners Manual.* New York: W. W. Norton.

Sack, Allen and Ellen Staurowsky. 1988. *College Athletes for Hire: The Evolution and Legacy of the NCAA's Amateur Myth.* Westport, CT: Praeger.

Sage, George. 1990. *Power and Ideology in American Sport: A Critical Perspective.* Champaign, IL: Human Kinetics Books.

Salter, David. 1996. *Crashing the Old Boys' Network: The Tragedies and Triumphs of Girls and Women in Sports.* Westport, CT: Praeger.

Schumpeter, Joseph. 1989 [1951]. *Essays: On Entrepreneurs, Innovations, Business Cycles, and the Evolution of Capitalism.* New Brunswick, NJ: Transaction Publishers.

Sherif, Muzafer, O. J. Harvey, B. Jack White, William Hood and Carolyn Sherif. 1988. *The Robbers Cave Experiment: Intergroup Conflict and Cooperation.* Middletown, CT: Wesleyan University Press.

Shropshire, Kenneth. 1990. *Agents of Opportunity: Sports Agents and Corruption in Collegiate Sports.* Philadelphia: University of Pennsylvania Press.

Valentine, Charles. 1968. *Culture and Poverty: Critique and Counter Proposals.* Chicago: University of Chicago Press.

Wallerstein, Immanuel. 1983. *Historical Capitalism.* London: Verso.

Wenner, Lawrence. 1989. "The Super Bowl Pregame Show: Cultural Fantasies and Political Subtext." in Wenner, Lawrence [ed.], *Media Sports and Society.* London: Sage.

Wilkerson, Martha and Richard Doddler. 1987. "Collective Conscience and Sport in Modern Society: An Empirical Test of a Model." *Journal of Leisure Research.* 19:35–40.

Zweigenhaft, Richard and William Domhoff. 1998. *Diversity in the Power Elite: Have Women and Minorities Reached the Top?* New Haven: Yale University Press.

6 Studying College and Society: A Field Guide

The previous chapters highlighted some ways that college society reflects social processes operating in the wider social arena. Rather than relying on a single theory, I adopted a variety of perspectives to illustrate the complexity of college life, as well as the wide range of sociological observations that can be made about society. These observations inform us not only about the social forces operating in colleges and universities, but also about how these forces operate in other institutions such as businesses, nations, and even in the world system. In this introduction to the sociological imagination, my hopes have been to not only inform the uninitiated about sociology, but also to create sociologists.

As a field guide to sociological research, this chapter offers some guideposts to help beginning researchers find their way from the initial formation of a research idea to the eventual collection and analysis of data. The issues presented here are commonly the subjects of entire courses, which will necessarily offer much more detailed instructions on methodology. These courses are commonly restricted to students who major in sociology, and are taken when students reach their junior or senior year in college. I think this unfortunate, because the best way to become a sociologist is by doing sociology and by engaging in the study of society. The sooner one begins studying society through some type of methodic system, the greater the potential for the development of a sociological imagination, as well as an appreciation for the joys (and travails) of being a sociologist.

The preceding chapters demonstrated that issues of sociological concern permeate college society. As a consequence, membership in the college community, particularly for students and faculty, offers access to an environment where one can study a wide range of pervasive social processes. Also, by virtue of the comparatively simple methods sociologists use, limited financial resources or a lack of experience will not necessarily present insurmountable barriers to new researchers studying what transpires in colleges and universities. So long as budding sociologists are willing to be perseverant, and have the foresight to apply the appropriate methodology to address their research questions, they stand a very good chance of producing sound sociological insights. The main concern for new sociologists is simply identifying manageable research projects and learning the tricks of the trade, the tried and tested methods used by sociologists in the study of society.

Sociological Methods and Folk Methods

It is a truism that all members of society are sociologists, in that everybody engages in some degree of analysis as they make sense out of their social experiences. This observation was forcefully revealed in a set of studies Harold Garfinkel performed with his students, detailed in his book *Studies in Ethnomethodology* (1967). Garfinkel termed his project a study in **ethnomethodology,** in that it was an examination of the folk (ethno) methods people use to understand their experiences. Garfinkel believed that society doesn't just exist; it is created and sustained by the assumptions people use in everyday encounters.

Garfinkel used an innovative approach to study these assumptions: rather than watching people as they customarily behaved, he deliberately disrupted the social world as it customarily operated. He showed, through a series of **breaching experiments,** that by breaching, or breaking the flow of normal interaction, it was possible to reveal how people make sense of, and rebuild, their social world. In one such experiment, Garfinkel asked his students to return to their dorm rooms and act as complete strangers to their roommates. Rather than behaving in a fashion typical of the student role, his students knocked on their own doors, asked permission before getting a snack from their refrigerators, and behaved just as a stranger would. As expected, by changing their roles, the students created encounters that would not have otherwise occurred. What happened?

First, it seemed apparent that all the roommates attempted to arrive at an explanation for the students' new manner of interacting. Some attributed it to being some kind of joke, others believed it indicated that the student was angry with them, and others thought that they were seeing symptoms of drug use or mental instability. Second, once a definition was created, the roommates acted accordingly. If the roommates thought it was a joke, they responded with laughter; anger definitions were responded to with hostility; and mental breakdown definitions stimulated roommates to express concern and offer guidance. Third, even after these responses, all the roommates then attempted to make the students return to their old behavior patterns. Being frustrated in these efforts, the roommates eventually either tried to avoid the student (hoping that the student would be more normal when they returned) or adamantly demanded that the student behave in the manner to which they were accustomed (i.e., "Stop it or else!").

Although not necessarily Garfinkel's intent, the study of ethnomethodology in many ways reaffirms the need for sociologists to use rigorous methodological approaches in the study of society, and that the folk methods that people (such as the roommates) use to understand social behavior should not be relied on. One shortcoming of folk methods of understanding society is that people tend to live in a **world-taken-for-granted** (Schutz 1932/1967). As long as events are happening in their customary ways, people seldom question the processes that create these patterns of behavior. For example, in Garfinkel's breaching experiment, it was only after the flow of normal social conduct was broken that the roommates reflected on the students' conduct. In contrast, the usual occurrence of events is one of the primary interests of sociologists, in that we are interested in figuring out how society works the way it does.

Another insight offered by Garfinkel's studies is that people act on the basis of explanations of social behavior that are not necessarily carefully examined. This was observed in the roommates' creation of new definitions of the situation and how their new observations were filtered through these definitions. People also tend to be reluctant to alter their definitions of reality even in light of contradictory evidence. In the case of the above study, the roommates tended to adopt one explanation for the students' peculiar behavior, not testing the merits of multiple different explanations in a systematic way.

Other studies in ethnomethodology reveal that people tend to collect experiences, not hard data. Nonsystematic personal observation limits "data" to the bounded experiences of what people customarily see and hear. As a consequence, individuals do not collect much information about social groups whose experiences run counter to their own. For example, as a consequence of limited experience, privileged students at Ivy League colleges will likely have little insight into what life is like for the rural poor, and the rural poor have little idea of what life is like at an Ivy League college. Lacking this information, both groups will tend to rely on **stereotypes,** unrefined and often uninformed depictions of groups different from their own. Once a stereotype is accepted, the tendency is to pay attention only to observations that fit this definition of reality and ignore observations that run counter to it.

In sum, the folk methods used by ordinary people work well enough for individuals as they negotiate their interactions with other people in everyday encounters. However, they are an inadequate means to obtain a rigorously informed understanding of how society operates. Sociology would be on shaky ground if the discipline operated this way. Sociologists would not be inclined to ask the types of questions that need to be examined, nor would they explore issues thoroughly enough to arrive at sound conclusions. Instead, sociologists need to create and use methods that enable them to accurately assess the complexity and diversity of the social world.

Sociology as a Science

Most sociologists consider themselves to be social *scientists* and try to adapt the approaches used in the study of the physical world to the study of the social world. As scientists, sociologists share a conviction that understanding is generated through an adherence to **empiricism** and that knowledge is gained primarily through systematic observation. Scientists are not content with untested opinion or any other assertion that is not accompanied by some form of data. When faced with opposing opinions, the opinion that has undergone the rigors of empirical tests is the opinion that is valued. Scientists also value **reason,** the use of logic and rational thought to connect empirical observations with one another. Data do not speak for themselves and knowledge does not fall off trees like apples, simply waiting to be collected. It takes critical thinking skills to make sense of the information collected and it takes critical thinking skills to develop the best means of collecting relevant data. By connecting reason with empiricism, sociologists are able to test theories and develop ever more informed understandings of how the society operates. This is science as it is ideally practiced, but unfortunately physical and social scientists have sometimes deviated from these principles.

In 1918, Max Weber offered a speech entitled "Science as a Vocation" to the students of Munich University (Gerth and Mills 1948/1991). Weber expressed concern that social scientists were mixing their politics with their research and that some lectures and publications were unreasonably biased to legitimate political positions. Weber argued that this type of political intrusion, if left unchecked, could threaten sociology's potential for advancing knowledge of society, and that it could simply become a tool for propaganda. To guard against this and other problems, Weber offered some advice concerning the disposition scientists should adopt in their research and teaching. His advice is as relevant today as it was then.

Weber advised social scientists to model their attitude to correspond with the disposition adopted by physical scientists. Part of this attitude stems from the high value scientists place on curiosity and the pursuit of new discoveries. In the physical sciences, scientists tend to be much more interested in learning about the unknown than in reaffirming what they already do know. If sociology is to be a science, Weber said it should be **void driven** and be comprised of people committed to finding out new things in new ways. Science is also a cumulative endeavor, with new insights built on the insights generated by past research. Scientists understand that they stand on the shoulders of the scientists who preceded them, and that each generation of researchers adds new discoveries to the collective body of knowledge. Weber argued that good social scientists are appreciative of the work of those who came before and learn about their findings and methods. By performing literature reviews and by learning about other studies, researchers learn the paths to making new discoveries. By reporting their findings, scientists contribute to the collective understanding of the processes that create the social and physical world.

Sociology is especially challenging to practice in a scientific manner because, left unchecked, values tend to intrude into the collection and analysis of data. As point of contrast, consider that a chemist is unlikely to have any feelings about, or personally identify with, a molecule. When the chemist studies the molecule, she will not develop an emotional relationship with the molecule, feel a need to advocate on the molecule's behalf, or worry about what the molecule might think of her. However, sociologists commonly feel these types of emotions when they study people. Recognizing this tendency, Weber suggested that sociologists adopt a position of **value neutrality** when engaged in research. Value-neutral research, or dispassioned analysis, involves setting one's own emotions and politics aside when entering into research endeavors. Weber never saw *Star Trek*, but if he had, he probably would have appreciated Mr. Spock as an exemplar of the value-neutral scientist, with logic and reason guiding the analysis, not politics or passions. This is not to say that values are divorced from science, only that they intersect with our research acts in a different manner. Our values determine what we study, according to Weber's concept of **value relevance,** but they do not determine what we will find. In American society, for instance, a high premium is placed on the need to locate, punish, and rehabilitate criminals. This same culture places a much lower premium on the arts. As a consequence, funding for criminological research is much more plentiful than funding for sociological studies of the arts, and there are many more sociological studies of crime than of music.

In studying college society, the distinction of value neutrality from value relevance bears considering. Budding sociologists will be most inclined to study groups of people that they have a strong interest in, as well as groups to which they belong. Athletes may be interested in doing sociological studies of sports on campus, lesbians may be interested in studying issues of gender and sexuality in college society, and Greeks may be interested in sororities and fraternities. Other times, interests will be sparked by current events, such as proposals to repeal affirmative action programs. Taking the latter as an example, the concept of value relevance suggests that it is entirely reasonable that a white male student be interested in studying affirmative action policies, especially if the student thinks that the program affects him or society in a negative way. In that affirmative action programs have been the subject of debate, and because affirmative action runs counter to the American values of individualism, the research topic has value relevance. Let us suppose that the student does not dislike blacks, Hispanics, Native Americans, or women, but he does have a strong dislike of a social program that he feels undermines his interests, as well as the interests of society as a whole. Here is the problem, how does he keep his own feelings and motivations from biasing his research?

Weber's approach to sociological research suggests that the young man adopt the disposition of a scientist, not the attitude of politician preparing for a debate. If our researcher sets out at the beginning with the sole intent of "proving" that affirmative action policies are bad, his approach will be to selectively collect data that supports his predetermined conclusion. Although his findings could be used to advance his political agenda, they probably would not offer much to advance our understanding of how this particular social program affects social behavior or the structure of society. After all, an equally motivated advocate of affirmative action programs could do the exact same thing and selectively report only data that support affirmative action programs. On the other hand, if he (or the advocate) conducts himself according to the rigors of the scientific disciplines, he will frame his research questions carefully. He will not focus on the conclusions he wants to support but rather on the questions that need to be answered and voids that need to be filled. For example, does affirmative action undermine or enhance college race relations? Has affirmative action increased the enrollment and post-college employment of minority students? What are the attitudes toward affirmative action on campus and how do they differ by race, gender, socioeconomic status, and age? Once a question is established, this researcher must then carefully design a rigorous study, conforming to the demands of his particular question. He must commit himself to the impartial collection and analysis of data and be open to the possibility that his initial beliefs may not be altogether correct. If practiced in a value-neutral manner, the findings of the study should come out the same, irrespective of the political orientation of the researcher.

Forming Research Questions

Arguably, the single most important step in a research project is determining the research question. Once properly constructed, the research question guides the selection of the methodology and focuses the data collection efforts. Often, however, people do not think in terms of questions, they think in terms of topics. Consider, for example, if I defined a potential study as "I want to study marijuana on college campuses." At this point, my research project is defined by a topic, not a question, and it remains unclear what I plan to find out about marijuana use. For example, I could be interested in distribution networks, pathways to becoming a marijuana user, drug treatment programs, or the social-psychological effects of marijuana use. Given the fact that it is unlikely that I can ever learn everything there is to know about marijuana on campus, my data collection efforts will necessarily be endless, as well as insufficient. In contrast, this study can become much more focused if I phrase my topic in terms of a research question. For example:

> How does marijuana use affect academic success?
> Does marijuana have an effect on psychological well-being?
> What types of biographical events lead one to becoming a marijuana user?
> Are there variations in marijuana use among different college campuses?
> How is marijuana distributed on campus?

Not only do these questions make apparent what I will be studying, they also help create a clearer vision of the data that I will need to collect.

In structuring research questions, sociologists need to use circumspection and consider the demands that a question will place upon themselves and their subjects. For example, I would probably discourage students from doing a study on marijuana distribution networks on a college campus, unless they could demonstrate that their research activities would not put themselves or their subjects at risk. Likewise, studying the variation in marijuana use between campuses would likely require resources of time and money (for travel) that many new researchers lack. Thus questions need to be formed in a way that anticipates empirical, financial, and ethical concerns.

Conceptualizing

After a research question is formed, researchers need to think carefully about the concepts that will be assessed in their study. This is accomplished through **conceptualization,** the process whereby vaguely understood notions are clearly delineated and defined for the purposes of measurement. To illustrate importance of conceptualization, let us pose another research question: How does intelligence affect success in college society? This is probably a "doable" research question, but it poses a thorny problem, in that it necessitates measuring "intelligence" and "success." Resolving this concern involves refining these abstract ideas and constructing indicators that can gauge the degree to which they are present.

The first step in this process is to create a **nominal definition,** an explicit statement that defines a term. In the case of the controversial book *The Bell Curve,* Herrnstein and Murray (1994) defined intelligence in accordance with a long tradition of psychometric research, as being comprised of primary mental abilities. These mental abilities were thought of as indicating an overarching indication of general intelligence, or "g," that can be used to compare individuals with one another.

Once a nominal definition is constructed, researchers then operationalize the concept. An **operational definition** is an explicit statement of how the concept is to be measured. For Herrnstein and Murray, intelligence was operationalized in accordance with the Stanford-Binet intelligence test. This instrument uses questions designed to measure verbal, quantitative, and spatial reasoning skills. Scores on these questions are centered against age-based group averages to produce an intelligence quotient (IQ). This standardized measurement of intelligence enables researchers to compare individuals, as well as compare the intelligence of different social groups according to the same standards. Because Murray and Herrnstein's subsequent analysis rests on the validity of conceptualizing intelligence as IQ, they provide an entire chapter of *The Bell Curve* to legitimate its use.

Herrnstein and Murray demonstrated that IQs are a fairly strong predictor of academic and economic success and that IQs vary by socioeconomic status and ethnicity. Correspondingly, the authors concluded that the reason why some ethnic groups tend to be disproportionately poor, criminal, or poorly educated, is that they lack the intelligence to do better. This finding is presented in relation to African Americans, who score on average nearly 20 points lower on IQ tests than whites do, which Herrnstein and Murray use to lend credence to an assertion that blacks are less intelligent than whites. They further assert that these lower IQ scores explain why African Americans are less likely to be successful in college and society. Although Herrnstein and Murray tried to skirt the issue of what causes blacks to have lower IQs, it is quite clear in their presentation that they attribute much of this difference to biological (genetic) causes.

A number of critics, spanning a variety of disciplines, raised concerns about the analytic methods and findings presented in *The Bell Curve* (see Fraser 1995). One concern is causal: whether it is IQs that cause economic attainment, or whether it is economic standing that influences the formation of an IQ. Setting this issue aside, other concerns arise from conceptualizing intelligence as IQ. An alternate approach, advanced by Howard Gardner (1995), defines intelligence in a fundamentally different way. Gardner's thesis centers on the idea of multiple intelligences and that IQ tests do not measure all of the dimensions of what we really understand "intelligence" to be. For example, IQ tests do not capture musical intelligence (i.e., the ability to perform or compose music), personal intelligence (i.e., the ability to work with other people and know oneself), or bodily-kinesthetic skills (the ability to perform in athletics or dance). Because IQ scores do not measure these things, many types of intelligence are effectively glossed over in *The Bell Curve*. Gardner suggests that intelligence can be conceptualized in a very different way, as the ability to solve real-world problems with dexterity. Who can write a lyric opera? Who can design a rocket engine? Who can shoot a basketball at half court? Who can work in a legislature to craft a new law? Who can take an infant and raise it to be a happy child? To a great extent, a person's intelligence in the real world is not measured by their capacities to do a pencil-and-paper IQ test but rather by their abilities to deal with real-world problems, problems that may change in remarkable ways throughout the life course.

The implications of Gardner's conceptualization and research led his thinking and policy recommendations in a decidedly different direction from Herrnstein and Murray. *The Bell Curve* concludes with an argument to eliminate college programs intended to advance minority students' success. These programs are portrayed as wasteful expenditures of money that could better be spent on students who have greater capacities for college success. On the other hand, Gardner (1983) suggests that we rethink the ways we teach students, with an understanding that people do not necessarily approach problems in the same way. He also suggests that we be sensitive to the fact that not all students have been given the opportunity to develop skills needed to cope in the college environment. Rather than pulling away from student support services, Gardner's conceptualization of intelligence leads him to the exact opposite conclusion from Herrnstein and Murray!

The Bell Curve and related debates reveal that the merits of any study are tightly coupled with the ways in which abstract ideas are codified into measures. All subsequent analysis rests on the degree to which researchers are able to create ways of accurately measuring conceptualizations of behaviors, circumstances, or events. Once an idea is conceptualized, it is possible for scholars to understand the strengths and limitations of any particular study, as well as link studies with one another. It also makes it possible to collect data appropriate to the research question.

Selecting a Methodology

Over the past century and a half of sociological research, sociologists have developed a number of methodologies specifically designed to study social relationships. Most sociological studies use one of four different methodologies: surveys, experiments, field observation, and unobtrusive observation. These are instruments in the sociological tool kit, ways of measuring social relationships. The question for the budding sociologist concerns which approach is the most appropriate for his or her research project. As the following discussion reveals, each method offers particular advantages in studying society, as well as limitations. The selection of a method is a concern of linking the right measurement strategies with the research question being addressed.

Surveys

Surveys are especially good techniques to use in the study of college society because they are inexpensive, easily distributed, and can provide data in a short period of time. They can take multiple forms and can be conducted with pencil and paper, via the Internet, over the telephone, or in face to face interviews. Surveys can also be designed to collect **quantitative data** (statistical information) or **qualitative data** (discursive information). As a rule, quantitatively designed surveys are easier to analyze and report, but qualitative surveys offer richer descriptive information about particular circumstances in people's lives. In general, surveys are best suited for capturing accounts of attitudes and experiences, and as such provide a useful means of capturing the range of perspectives and behaviors in society.

Given the wide variety of surveys, which type of survey is the best for doing sociological research in college society? The short answer is that it depends on the research question and the resources available to the researcher. For example, college administrators tend to favor quantitative pencil-and-paper surveys as a means of assessing student attitudes about professors and courses. Typically these are formatted so they can be immediately scanned into computers and results quickly compiled into statistical summaries. While these instruments offer many advantages, pen-and-paper teaching evaluations do a poor job of generating rich qualitative accounts of the subjective experience of being in a class and detailing particular moments that delight or frustrate students. A similar approach could also be used to obtain information on the fad of tattooing. Students could be asked to report the number of tattoos they have, when they obtained these body modifications, and their intents to have more tattoos, as well as to report demographic information such as age, sex, and family socioeconomic status. These pen-and-paper instruments would be less adept at capturing the reasons why students choose to get tattooed and why they chose one particular tattoo over another. The latter questions would favor in-depth, face-to-face interviews, which allow the researchers to probe the respondents, asking for detailed information about the circumstances surrounding their decisions and experiences.

Surveys also vary on the degree to which they are standardized. **Standardized surveys** follow a protocol that is stipulated at the outset, with question phrasings and sequences predetermined. Most quantitative interviews and questionnaires are highly standardized. An obvious advantage of this practice is that respondents are all treated in an identical manner, and therefore their responses can be compared with one another. A cost, however, is that the interview is like a grilling session, leaving little or no room for a respondent to offer information that is not otherwise requested. **Unstandardized surveys** (almost exclusively qualitative in nature) do not mandate a discreet ordering of questions and do not require a strict adherence to question phrasing. While these types of interviews flow like a conversation, analysis is more difficult and comparisons of one subject's responses with another's must be done with greater caution. Another alternative is to develop a **semistandardized interview.** In this circumstance, questions are predetermined and phrasings of specific questions carefully developed, but the protocol offers the researcher considerable discretion on the ordering of questions and the latitude to probe respondents when interesting information is uncovered during the interview. The choice of a highly standardized, semistandardized, or unstandardized interview format depends on the nature of the research question. If there is little existing information on a research topic, unstandardized interviews can be conducted with justification. In general, though, studies using survey methods will be better received if they follow a rigorous procedure of collecting information and follow a semistandardized or highly standardized interview guide.

Conducting a survey requires great care in phrasing questions so that the researcher is able to collect the information needed, as well as maintain rapport with the respondents. Ideally all questions should be phrased so that respondents will be forthcoming in offering honest responses to the researcher's inquiries. Toward this end, questions should not be biased, or influence the respondent to affirm any particular response. For example, asking respondents a leading question such as "Don't you think that peer pressure plays some role in a person's decision to get tattooed?" may direct participants to answer in the affirmative. Questions should also not be "double-barreled"—asking two or more questions simultaneously. For example, it would be inadvisable to ask "Do you think that tattoo parlors should be open only to adults and that people should not be allowed to get tattoos when they are visibly under the influence of drugs or alcohol?" An answer of "no" to this question would still be unclear, leaving the researcher to wonder if this means no to both questions or to only one of the questions asked. Also, in that face-to-face surveys necessitate the maintenance of rapport, interviewers are well advised to offer sensitive phrasings of questions. For example, stating a question as "Why did you get that tattoo?" could put some respondents on the defensive, especially if they suspected that the researcher is not sympathetic to their decision to get a tattoo. On the other hand, "Could you tell me about your decision to get a tattoo— how did you finally decide that you wanted to get one?" offers the subject a more open and nonjudgmental line of inquiry (see Berg 2001).

Surveys are useful, but they have many limitations. One concern is that this methodology relies on the honesty and insight of respondents as they offer accounts of their own behavior. In reality, responses often do not mesh well with other measures of respondents' actual experiences. For example, by comparing the information provided by ex-patients with information recorded in medical records, one study revealed that 58% of the patients gave inaccurate information about their length of stay in a hospital, 23% were inaccurate about the month of discharge, 35% about the diagnosis, 25% about the type of surgery, and 10% were inaccurate about whether surgery had been performed (reported in Reinharz 1979). Another concern with this methodology is that surveys can give a false impression of society. This is particularly evident in the case of quantitatively oriented surveys that portray an overly clean vision of what is in reality a complex world. For example, our hypothetical questionnaire on tattoos may ask a question such as "Would you say that you are very happy, somewhat happy, somewhat unhappy, or very unhappy that you got a tattoo." All respondents will be able to check one of those four boxes on a self-administered questionnaire. In reality, respondents' attitudes towards their decision to have a tattoo may be much more complicated than this question will reveal. Perhaps happiness may have little to do with the disposition one takes toward a tattoo, which may be linked with other concerns such as hostility towards parents and authority figures, or desires to fit into particular subcultures. In the descriptive account of the-world-presented-through-pen-and-paper-survey-research, though, many of these complexities are glossed over (Reinharz 1979). This is not to say that surveys are of little value, only that they have limitations and should only be used when they are appropriate to the research question being studied.

Unobtrusive Observation

Sociologists are always interested in measurement, and sometimes we apply our techniques even to issues outside our formal research activities. For example, at the beginning of all my classes I send around a brief survey, asking students to sign in (providing a measure of attendance) and to signify whether they had read the previous night's assignment (providing an indication of preparedness). On one fateful day our class assignment was to read a chapter from *Nonreactive Measures in the Social Sciences* (Webb, Campbell, Schwartz, Sechrest, and Grove 1981), which I had photocopied and posted at the reserve desk of the library. Even though my survey of attendance/preparedness indicated that all my students had read the assignment and were prepared to discuss it, I was astonished that none of my students seemed able to offer an intelligent response to even the most basic question about the reading. "What could be happening?" I wondered. At the end of the semester, I received my reserve readings back from the library. As I sorted through these packets, I noticed a curious thing. Unlike the photocopied reading assignments given earlier in the semester, there was not a single comment scribbled in the margins of these photocopies. In fact, where the pages were stapled together, there wasn't even a crease showing that the pages had been turned. My students had deceived me on my survey; none of them had read the assignment!

My "findings" reaffirmed what was suggested in *Nonreactive Measures in the Social Sciences*, that oftentimes the best way to measure social behavior is not by asking people about their opinions or conduct, but rather by looking at the traces that they leave behind as they engage in human conduct. People commonly produce artifacts that indicate their values and their behaviors.

The trick for the sociologist is to develop systematic methods of measuring these artifacts. For example, determining how much alcohol students consume could be measured by examining cash register receipts at liquor stores, and by comparing alcohol sales when school is in and out of session. Another unobtrusive method, that could address this same issue, is to count the number of beer and liquor bottles in student garbage cans. In both instances, the information gained could actually offer more accurate measures of alcohol consumption than would be revealed in interviews with students, who could overestimate or underestimate how much they consume.

The chief empirical advantage of unobtrusive methods is that they are **nonreactive.** Unlike most other methodologies, the unobtrusive measurement of social behavior has no effect on the people being studied, and as a result subjects do not have the opportunity to deceive or put up a front. In addition, unobtrusive methods offer logistical advantages, in that they tend to be inexpensive and expedient.

There are a wide variety of unobtrusive data-gathering techniques, but most unobtrusive studies fall into one of two strategies: content analysis and archival research. **Content analysis** involves the systematic coding of traces of human values and behavior. So long as people produce things, it is possible to collect these things for the purpose of study. Not only can the content of garbage cans be studied to determine alcohol consumption, wear on floor tiles can determine patterns of traffic, graffiti on bathroom walls can reveal personal interests, and lyrics in songs can reveal cultural values (to name but a few possible sources of data). Studying content involves developing a **coding scheme,** a systematic catalogue of the artifacts left behind. For example, at its simplest level, a coding scheme of the content of graffiti from bathroom walls would be a list of each piece of graffiti and a record of where that graffiti came from (i.e., a men's room or a women's room). This information could be used to provide tallies of who are more likely to leave graffiti on bathroom walls, men or women. It could also be used to illustrate the types of graffiti that occur in each room (Farr and Gordon 1975; Smith 1988).

Good content analyses report the substance of the data in two ways: in terms of its manifest content and its latent content. Simply reporting verbatim what is written in graffiti would constitute an analysis of the **manifest content,** a surface description of the artifacts. On the other hand, **latent content** examines the deep underlying meanings that are revealed in these traces. The study of latent content requires attuning oneself to the subtleties of the artifacts, looking carefully at what they reveal about social sentiments and values. For example, men's room walls are commonly adorned with homoerotic messages, and sometimes these messages state a specific time to meet for sexual relations. On a manifest level, these graffiti simply constitute messages advertising for sexual contact. This interpretation, though, would likely be inaccurate, given that an open signal of a desire to engage in public sex could be very risky. With this acknowledged, it becomes clear that what is manifest is not really the important content of the graffiti. On a latent level, these graffiti constitute a means for participants in "the tearoom trade" to mark particular bathrooms for public sex, sending other willing participants signals that this environment may lead to successful encounters (Humphreys 1970). Commonly these messages are also accompanied with a dialogue of graffiti written by others, such as the graffiti scrawled in the bathroom near my former office stating "DIE FAG." On the surface, graffiti are just statements written on bathroom walls. On a deeper level, they comprise ways for groups to stake out territories, claim social spaces, and legitimate or challenge alternate lifestyles (Smith 1998).

Colleges and universities provide a great deal of content that can be analyzed. For example, textbooks can be analyzed for their depiction of ethnic minorities in both photographs and in textual descriptions (Shaw-Taylor and Benokraitis 1995). Cultural values also can be determined by analyzing song lyrics obtained from personal CD and record collections (Sweet 1996). Content is literally limitless on college campuses, and with a little creativity, new and interesting research studies can be constructed.

Another approach to doing unobtrusive research is through analysis of **archival records.** This involves studying statistics that have already been collected for other purposes, and exploring them in relation to new research questions. As a matter of course, bureaucracies store detailed records of their operations, and college society is no exception. For instance, admissions offices commonly keep track of enrollment, application rates, and incoming students' SAT scores, gender, and racial background. Registrars' offices track student grades, course loads, graduation rates, and number of majors. Career service offices often track student placement in the job market following graduation. Campus police record the number of complaints and arrests on campus. All of these data can be potentially linked with one another and can be exploited for research purposes. For example, when I served on a campus task force to study fraternity pledging, I compiled a list of students who had pledged fraternities and sororities, along with the year they pledged. I provided this list to the registrar and had her produce a comparison of student grade point averages, comparing Greek and non-Greek GPAs. I found (much to my surprise) that grades among potential Greek members did not decline during pledging, but that they did decline significantly the semester following pledging.

Archival analysis offers a great advantage in that much of the data collection efforts have already been performed before the researcher even begins his or her study. There are some concerns, though, researchers should keep in mind when using archived data. One concern is availability, and that one can only study what is accessible. Bureaucracies tend to be reluctant to share information to outsiders. However, because students and faculty are members of their college society, they may be in an advantageous position to access data that might otherwise be kept secret. Seeking information is not always successful, though. For example, even though colleges have precise data on faculty salaries, this information tends to be a closely guarded secret. The same is true with student grade point averages, which will not necessarily be released to other students and faculty.

Researchers also have to satisfy themselves with the data that are collected, and are not in control of determining the detail or precision of this information. As such, studies tend to be limited to studying the types of information that bureaucrats find of interest, which will sometimes be insufficient for research purposes. Researchers also need to be wary of the reliability and validity of data. For example, even if one does get access to campus police records, one can not necessarily trust that these records accurately indicate the degree of crime on campus. There are a number of factors that may bias these data. For example, even if campus police reports indicate no rapes on campus, this does not necessarily mean that no rapes occurred, only that no rapes were reported or written down.

Experiments

Experimental studies involve structuring carefully controlled situations in order to test if a particular stimulus has an effect on subsequent behavior. This is sociology's closest approximation of the methodologies used in the physical sciences. Because researchers control the exposure to the stimuli, experiments can be a highly effective means of resolving debates that center on concerns of causality, whether one event actually causes another event to occur.

In contrast to unobtrusive measures, experiments tend to be very intrusive. Subjects in experiments are usually formally recruited, put in laboratory situations, exposed to a particular event or stimulus, and their subsequent behavior carefully measured. Their behavior is then contrasted with subjects in a **control group,** a set of subjects who are exposed to as many elements in the experiment as possible, with the exception of exposure to the stimulus in question. In many sociological experiments, it is not always possible to include a true control group. Instead, studies are commonly designed to include **comparison groups,** groups that are exposed to different levels of the stimulus.

Burwell (1987) outlines a classic sociological experiment, the "lost letter technique," and demonstrates the ease with which it can be applied to the study of social behavior on campus. The lost letter technique involves strategically dropping self-addressed envelopes around campus. Because the only way the letters will find their way back to the researcher is by people picking them up and placing them in a mailbox, it offers a means of understanding the factors that influence people to engage in altruistic behavior. Essential to this study is a careful manipulation of factors that could potentially influence altruism. One possibility is manipulating the socioeconomic status of the recipient of the altruistic act, which can be accomplished through the addresses on the envelopes. For example, some letters could be addressed to a high-status individual (i.e., "Professor John Jones") and others to a low-status individual (i.e., "John Jones, Assistant Janitor"). If altruism is affected by social status, it is logical to expect to see the envelopes being returned at different rates. One could also study if greater help is extended to women than men by manipulating the gender on the address. Another possibility for applying this technique could involve manipulating the locations in which letters are dropped. For example, a researcher could arrange for friends on other campuses to drop letters as well, opening the possibilities for studying the effects of urban versus rural campuses on helping behavior (see also Hansson and Slade 1977; Milgram 1970).

As researchers think about implementing experiments, they need to keep in mind a few logistical and empirical concerns. Conducting experiments can be very time consuming, and it is often difficult to generate willing subjects unless there is some type of reward offered for participating. Laboratory experiments also tend to be contrived, and thus subjects are studied in situations that bear only modest similarities to the ways in which real-world encounters are normally structured. This concern implies that researchers need to use considerable care when generalizing the findings of experiments to explain behaviors that occur outside the laboratory.

It is also important to keep in mind that subjects often behave differently as soon as they know that they are being experimented upon, a concern commonly referred to as the **Hawthorne effect.** The Hawthorne effect is named after the electric plant where a series of experiments were conducted on worker behavior that revealed a surprising finding. In manipulating factors such as lighting intensity and employee rest periods, researchers found that no matter which factor was manipulated, and no matter whether they increased or decreased the intensity or duration of that factor, productivity tended to increase. They concluded that it was not so much the factors in the study that were influencing behavior as much as it was simply being in the study itself. Although there has been some debate on whether the Hawthorne effect really occurred in the original study (Jones 1992), it is widely acknowledged that subjects tend to behave differently in situations where they know they are being experimented upon. This concern has to be taken into account when designing studies and interpreting results.

In some circumstances researchers lack the power to manipulate the variables hypothesized to affect behavior (i.e., the letters). In these instances, quasi-experimental designs can be of great help. A **quasi-experiment** is an "experimental-like" design, which accommodates the researcher's inability to randomly assign subjects to experimental conditions. For example, seldom can a researcher determine who will (or will not) be exposed to a new law or social policy. For example, researchers were in no position to determine when and where affirmative action programs were put in place, nor could they determine when and where they were to be dismantled. This doesn't mean, however, that the effects of affirmative action cannot be studied with a quasi-experimental methodology. In 1996, voters in the state of California, under Proposition 209, outlawed the consideration of race in admissions to state colleges. What effect did this have on the enrollments of minorities at California's prestigious state universities? One quasi-experimental approach is to track minority student enrollment before and after the implementation of proposition 209. The effects were startling at the University of California's three law schools, where the admission of African American students dropped by 63%, Native Americans by 60%, and Hispanics by 34%. At the same time, the admission of Asian students increased by 43%, and whites by 27% (Bronner 1998). If researchers can position their research around the time of the introduction of a new law or policy such as this, they can gauge its effects on social behavior.

In a handy little book, *Experimental and Quasi-Experimental Designs for Research*, Campbell and Stanley (1966) outline a number of experimental-like designs that can be implemented to determine the causes of social behavior. Quasi-experiments are unique in the approach of shaping research to react to social events, creating opportunities to test the impact of events on social behavior. Has your campus implemented a new program or policy? Has some dramatic event happened on campus, such as a natural disaster? These types of events constitute rare opportunities for sociologists. With some creativity, circumstances that are entirely beyond control can become some of the best opportunities for gauging the effects of events on social experiences (for further illustration, see Sweet 1998).

Field Observation

Another approach to doing research is observing people as they normally behave in their natural environments. These **field observations** enable researchers to gain a deep understanding of the ways in which individuals locate themselves relative to other individuals in society. It also enables us to write **thick descriptions** (Geertz 1973) of human conduct, detailed portraits of social encounters and assessments of what those encounters mean to the individuals participating in them. Students and faculty in college society are in an especially advantageous position to engage in field observation because of the flexibility in their schedules, as well as their access to observing different social groups on campus.

The field research of Michael Moffatt (1989) offers an illustration of the insights generated by crossing over into unfamiliar social groups on campus. Moffatt, a professor, posed as a new admission to Rutgers University. Playing the student role, he was placed in a dorm, assigned a roommate, and went through the rigors of registration and attending classes. By posing as an undergraduate student, Moffatt was able to observe classroom encounters from the students' perspective and listen to unguarded student comments about their professors.

Having served as a faculty member, Moffatt's experience as a "student" showed him that students often have a very different (and sometimes better) understanding of campus life than faculty, who tend to ignore such "peripheral" concerns as registration procedures or what other faculty members' classes are like. Moffatt found that students know that fellow students can offer very good information about which courses to avoid and how to negotiate one's way through the bureaucracy of college society. He found also something surprising to many faculty, something that academics actually rank very low in students' values. Instead, the students he interacted with tended to be much more concerned with negotiating successful sexual encounters, figuring out ways of obtaining alcohol and drugs, and establishing an identity and status among their peers in the dorms.

In field research projects such as this, sociologists have to be particularly concerned with their role in the social encounters, which can vary from marginal to full involvement with the group. One approach is to become a **complete participant,** and to be fully involved with the group activities. Complete participants keep their identity as sociologist secret, so that they are treated fully as group members. While this offers some advantages, it can limit researchers' ability to ask their subjects questions. Moffatt initially tried to be a complete participant in his study of college life, but one problem he soon faced was that students became suspicious of this older man's presence and apparent inquisitiveness. Why was he there? Why did he seem to know so much and yet be a student? Why does he ask such odd questions? The obvious answer was that he was a narcotics officer! Once defined as such, Moffatt had to redefine his presence to students and "come clean" as a social scientist.

Once Moffatt confessed that he was a sociologist occupying a student role, he redefined his position to that of a **participant observer.** Participant observers occupy a dual status in the eyes of their subjects, as a group member as well as a researcher. In many respects, the participant observer role is the most advantageous approach to doing field observation because it enables the researcher to observe subjects' behavior in a natural setting, as well as interview subjects and ask naïve questions. One other potential strategy is to become a **complete observer.** Complete observers keep their status as researcher secret from their subjects. They also avoid interacting with the group under study, and make observations covertly. This comprises the "fly on the wall" approach to doing field observation. Of the various methods of field observation, this method is the least intrusive but also tends to offer the least information and the most wasted time.

Field observation poses a number of challenges to researchers. Two such challenges are overcoming the reluctance of groups to being studied and gaining permission from **gatekeepers** to engage in observation. Campuses, for the most part, tend to be quite open to members of the campus community, but this is not always the case. For example, students who want to engage in a field observation study of faculty conduct on university committees would likely have to get permission from the provost's or the president's office. Nonmembers of the campus community would likely face even greater hurdles in bypassing gatekeepers. It is also important to recognize that field observation studies tend to be time consuming, often taking years simply in the collection of data. Field observation studies are also limited to very small samples, and as a result, create difficulties in generalizing the findings to explain the behavior of other groups who have not been studied.

Further Concerns: Sampling

In the year 2000 there are an estimated 15 million students and 2.5 million employees working in the 3706 colleges and universities in the United States (Statistical Abstract of the United States 1998). It is unlikely that any researcher will be able to study all of these schools, students, and employees. Lacking the ability to study everyone, research projects rest on generating reliable samples. **Sampling** offers a means of making studies feasible, by selecting representatives (usually people or organizations) that reflect the characteristics of the group under study. How does one generate a sample, though?

To formalize the discussion for a moment, consider that an **element** is the smallest unit of study and a **population** comprises the aggregate of all of the potential elements under study. The population of colleges and universities comprises all 3706 of these institutions. The State University of New York at Potsdam and Princeton University would comprise two elements in this population. The population of college students comprises all 15 million students in the United States, and each individual student would be an element. Given that in most circumstances we will not be able to study the entire population of colleges or students, what is the best approach to selecting elements (individual colleges or students) from these populations?

One approach is to simply take a **convenience sample** and study friends and associates where one works or resides. Unfortunately, oftentimes the people who are most convenient to study are the least representative of a population under study. For instance, in generating convenience samples, researchers will tend to study the people they know and thus select individuals who hold similar values and who share similar levels of access to resources. As a consequence, different researchers using this same sampling technique will likely generate very different portraits of the characteristics of the individuals or organizations in a society. Consider, for instance, if a research project concerned studying the level of funding for specific college programs, and one study was performed by a student at Princeton and the other by a student as SUNY Potsdam. If each student studied their own college and then used their findings to talk about the funding for college programs in the population of all colleges, they would likely come to very different conclusions and policy recommendations.

A more favorable approach is to structure a sampling strategy that is specifically designed to meet the needs of the research project. In many circumstances, research projects benefit from gaining a **representative sample,** a selection of elements that will reveal the characteristics of a population as a whole. One of the best ways of accomplishing this is to select subjects through a **random sample.** A random sample is generated by giving every potential element in a population an equal chance of being selected. For instance, one could use flips of a coin, rolls of a die, or draw names out of a hat as a means of selecting colleges, or individuals affiliated with colleges, for inclusion in a study. Another approach could be to engage in **systematic sampling,** whereby subjects are selected at predetermined intervals. For example, one could pick colleges by constructing a list of all colleges and selecting every fifth, tenth, or hundredth college on that list. Likewise, students could be selected for interviews by stopping every other person entering the student union. In both approaches, because the laws of probability are used to select subjects, they guard against intentional or unintentional researcher biases that would tend to favor some elements over others.

In other circumstances, it may be difficult to obtain lists of potential elements. For instance, if one sets out to study gay and lesbian students, it will likely be difficult to find information that would lead directly to members of this population. In such circumstances **snowball sampling** can be a helpful strategy. This approach involves making contact with a few initial subjects. After the interviews, the subjects are then asked to refer the researcher to a few more subjects in their network of relations. As this process is repeated for each subject, the sample size grows exponentially. Another approach, **purposive sampling,** involves deliberately selecting elements because they are likely to provide especially useful information. For example, a study of any particular college may benefit by deliberately including interviews with student government leaders or faculty administrators. Even though these individuals are not "typical," they are valuable to include because they know a great deal about the bureaucratic operations in the institution.

How big should a sample be? There is no firm answer to this question, but there are two rules of thumb that can guide one's thinking. Rule 1: The bigger the sample, the better the study. The more elements included in a sample, the greater the likelihood that the diversity of a population will be revealed. For example, if a researcher has only studied nineteen people, there is great potential for a twentieth subject to contribute new and useful information to the study. Rule 2: The law of diminishing returns. While there are tremendous gains in adding each new element to a small sample, once a sample becomes sufficiently large the amount gained by adding each new element decreases. Again, think of the benefits of adding one subject to a sample that already has five hundred subjects included. While subject 501 may add new information, this person will carry less weight in shaping the findings. For this reason, national polls that rely on samples of two thousand people can do nearly as good a job at estimating the characteristics of the population of the United States as polls that use four thousand people. In combining these two rules of thumb, in general it is best for researchers to design studies that have as large a sample as their resources (time and money) will reasonably permit, but also to limit their samples in accordance with the need to use resources in an effective manner.

Ethics and Social Research

Thus far, the designs of methodologies have been examined in relation to research questions and resources. Of even greater importance are the concerns of designing research projects that adhere to moral standards that uphold the dignity and well-being of research participants. The *American Sociological Association Code of Ethics* (1997) offers a set of guidelines that help researchers construct studies that will be considerate of the many potential ethical problems that are inherent in studying social relations.

To highlight just a few of these concerns, consider the ethical dilemma that confronted one researcher, and the response of two competing professional communities. While James Scarce was working on a study of radical political groups, members of the Animal Liberation Front (ALF) vandalized the animal research facilities at Washington State University, causing over $100,000 in damage, and an inestimable loss of scientific data. Although Scarce was not a suspect, he was subpoenaed to provide potentially incriminating evidence against the ALF, a group that prosecutors believed he was knowledgeable about as a result of his research. Scarce refused to surrender his field notes, stating that he had assured his subjects confidentiality. He was jailed after claiming professional responsibilities and rights similar to those commonly extended to news reporters. The arrest of Scarce prompted the American Sociological Association to file an amicus brief in support of his stance, arguing that sociological studies often require the assurance of confidentiality. They further stated that it was the moral obligation of researchers to stand by their promises, and that if Scarce was legally required to surrender his notes, it would undermine the ability of future sociologists to conduct research on deviant groups (Footnotes 1993). The Ninth Circuit Court of Appeals disagreed and found Scarce guilty of contempt (United States Court of Appeals 1993).

The case of James Scarce highlights some important concerns worthy of reflection. For instance, which should take precedence, the moral standards of a professional community or the moral standards present in society? How far must sociologists extend themselves to protect the well-being of their subjects? At what point can researchers break their promises? To what groups do sociologists have the greatest loyalties—their subjects, their profession, or society as a whole? The answers to these questions are not always clear.

In thinking about moral actions and research, Pescosolido (1991) suggests that ethics be thought about on three analytic hierarchies, micro level concerns, meso level concerns, and macro level concerns. On a micro level, sociologists have to concern themselves with moral conduct in relation to their subjects. In this respect the primary moral concern centers around protecting the well-being and dignity of anyone participating in the study. Commonly this is accomplished by assuring confidentiality and by not personally identifying any subject in the study report. The ASA also requires that subjects give informed consent, and that participation in research studies should be voluntary. There are exceptions, though. For instance, public records can be accessed and reported without the consent of subjects. The *ASA Code of Ethics* also prohibits the intentional harming of subjects who participate in studies. In the event that a study may negatively affect subjects, researchers are obligated to demonstrate that this risk is justified by appreciable social benefits.

At a meso level, sociologists are also expected to conduct themselves in a manner that upholds the dignity of their profession. For instance, researchers are expected to conduct themselves with decorum when debating other researchers who hold alternate stances on controversial topics. This stands in marked contrast to the climate that is cultivated on television talk shows, where he or she who shouts loudest wins. Even when sociologists seek to promote their own research, they are ethically obligated to do so in a manner that, above all, creates respect for the well-being of the profession of sociology. This professional morality concerns linking oneself with others engaged in the sociological enterprise and working to keep the profession alive and vital.

At a macro level, sociologists also have to concern themselves with linking their profession with the other professional communities outside of sociology. This involves cultivating productive relationships with legislators, military, police, religious organizations, entrepreneurs, educators, environmentalists, and all other groups that are vital to societal well-being. It is the moral obligation of sociologists to consider the needs of these organizations, as well as to inform outsiders of contributions that sociology can make to societal interests. For example, for short-term gains, prosecutors will be inclined to pressure sociologists to surrender field notes, as was done in the case of Richard Scarce. An unfortunate consequence of this use of sociological research is that it limits future studies of deviant groups. Although there certainly can be short-term gains by using sociologists as informants, in the long run our understanding of the social causes of crime will be undermined as a result.

Fortunately the *American Sociological Association Code of Ethics* outlines many of the potential ethical concerns that can arise from research studies and the professional standards of the discipline. While not structured to certify any project as ethical, careful study of this document can be sociologists' best insurance against creating unforeseen problems that result from their studies.

Conclusion

Obtaining resources, convincing subjects to participate, constructing reliable measures, and analyzing data can make sociological research a challenging endeavor. Doing this in an ethical manner creates additional obstacles. However, in comparison to some other disciplines, sociology is relatively open to newcomers and can be performed using rather simple techniques. It is my hope that the above discussion has kindled a sense of excitement about the discipline. Rather than feeling daunted, I hope readers are now saying to themselves "Hey, I can do that!". If armed with nothing more than a steadfast dedication to understanding how society operates, chances are they can.

The above discussion centered on issues and concerns that are likely to emerge in the process of doing sociological research. Toward this end, I have deliberately avoided discussing the "nuts-and-bolts" concerns of actually doing research, and instead offered a general overview of the dominant approaches used in sociological research. To help in the fine-tuning of methodological approaches, the references listed below can offer greater insight into the concerns and application of different research strategies. In the end, though, methodology is seldom seen as captivating or important until it is tied to real-world research applications. As research questions are applied to issues inside and outside of the college society, the need for methods and methodological expertise becomes apparent. Identifying and surmounting methodological challenges is one of the great rewards open to the imaginative sociologist as he or she applies the craft to the study of society.

REFERENCES

American Sociological Association. 1997. *American Sociological Association Code of Ethics. http:// www.asanet.org/members/ecoderev.html.*

Berg, Bruce. 2001. *Qualitative Research Methods for the Social Sciences (4th Edition)*. Boston: Allyn and Bacon.

Berger, Peter. 1963. *Invitation to Sociology: A Humanist Perspective*. Garden City, NY, Doubleday.

Bronner, Ethan. 1998. "Some Minority Admissions Drop in California." *New York Times*. January 14 p. B7.

Burwell, Ronald. 1987. "The Lost Letter Experiment: A Class Exercise for Research Methods." *Teaching Sociology.* 15:195–196.

Campbell, Donald and Julian Stanley. 1966. *Experimental and Quasi-Experimental Designs for Research.* Boston: Houghton Mifflin.

Farr, Jo-Ann and Carol Gordon. 1975. "A Partial Replication of Kinsey's Graffiti Study." *Journal of Sex Research.* 11:158–162.

Footnotes. 1993. Scarce Released from Jail. 21:1.

Fraser, Steven [ed.]. 1995. *The Bell Curve Wars: Race, Intelligence, and the Future of America.* New York: Basic Books.

Gardner, Howard. 1983. *Frames of Mind: The Theory of Multiple Intelligences.* New York: Basic Books.

Gardner, Howard. 1995. "Cracking Open the IQ Box" in Fraser, Steven [ed.]. *The Bell Curve Wars: Race, Intelligence, and the Future of America.* New York: Basic Books.

Garfinkel, Harold. 1967. *Studies in Ethnomethodology.* Englewood Cliffs: Prentice Hall.

Geertz, Clifford. 1973. *The Interpretation of Cultures: Selected Essays.* New York: Basic Books.

Gerth, Hans and C. Wright Mills. [1991] 1967. *From Max Weber: Essays in Sociology.* London: Routledge.

Hansson, Robert and Kenneth Slade. 1977. "Altruism Toward a Deviant in a City and a Small Town." *Public Opinion Quarterly.* 29:437–438.

Herrnstein, Richard and Charles Murray. 1994. *The Bell Curve: Intelligence and Class Structure in American Life.* New York: The Free Press.

Humphreys, Laud. 1970. *The Tearoom Trade: Impersonal Sex in Public Places.* Chicago: Aldine.

Jones, Stephen. 1992. "Was There A Hawthorne Effect?" *American Journal of Sociology.* 98:451–468.

Milgram, Stanley. 1970. "The Experience of Living in Cities." *Science.* 167:1461–1468.

Mills, C. Wright. 1959. *The Sociological Imagination.* New York: Oxford University Press.

Moffatt, Michael. 1989. *Coming of Age in New Jersey: College and American Culture.* New Brunswick, NJ: Rutgers University Press.

Pescosolido, Bernice. 1991. "The Sociology of the Professions and the Profession of Sociology: Professional Responsibility, Teaching, and Graduate Training." *Teaching Sociology.* 19:351–361.

Reinharz, Shulamit. 1979. *On Becoming a Social Scientist.* San Francisco: Jossey-Bass.

Schutz, Alfred. [1967] 1932. *The Phenomenology of the Social World.* Evanston, IL: Northwestern University Press.

Shaw-Taylor, Yoku and Nijole Benokraitis. 1995. "The Presentation of Minorities in Marriage and Family Textbooks." *Teaching Sociology.* 23:122–135.

Smith, George. 1998. "The Ideology of 'Fag': The School Experience of Gay Students." *Sociological Quarterly.* 39:309–335.

Statistical Abstract of the United States 1998. Washington, D.C: U.S. Department of Commerce.

Sweet, Stephen. 1996. "Bluegrass Music and Its Misguided Representation of Appalachia." *Popular Music and Society.* 20:37–51.

Sweet, Stephen. 1998. "The Effect of a Natural Disaster on Social Cohesion: A Longitudinal Study." *International Journal of Mass Emergencies and Disasters* 16:321–331.

United States Court of Appeals. 1993. *James Richard Scarce vs United States of America.* 93-35333. San Francisco: Barclays Law Publishers.

Webb, Eugene, Donald Campbell, Richard Schwartz, Lee Sechrest, and Janet Belew Grove. 1981. *Nonreactive Measures in the Social Sciences* (2nd Edition). Chicago: Rand McNally Press.

AFTERWORD

To be sure, sociology is an individual pastime in the sense that it interests some men and bores others.... But the word "pastime" is weak in describing what we mean. Sociology is more like a passion. The sociological perspective is more like a demon that drives one compellingly, again and again, to the questions that are its own. An invitation to sociology is, therefore, an invitation to a very special kind of passion. No passion is without its dangers. —Peter Berger, 1963. *Invitation to Sociology,* 1963

This book offered an introduction to the sociological imagination, using colleges to highlight the social forces that influence personal experience. Through the sociological lens, the condition of individuals working and studying in colleges and universities was framed in relation to the operations of society and the grand sweep of history. The perspectives and methods outlined in this book can be used not only to understand college life, but also to understand the many institutions that make up society. At its deepest level that is what this book was about: highlighting different ways to think about social experience and to invite readers to live a sociologically informed life.

I feel obligated, though, to close this book with words of caution, concerns I first learned about when I was an undergraduate reading Peter Berger's (1963) *Invitation to Sociology.* Berger warned that the sociological imagination offers a mixed blessing; that those intrigued with sociology tend to become absorbed with it. Even the most casual encounter can be framed through the sociological lens and there are few opportunities to escape "the social." The passion of sociology offers little room for a distraction from studying society and our place within the social order. This is, in part, why I chose to study college society. It is where I teach, where I research, and where I socialize. As a consequence, it became the thing I wanted to understand.

Beyond this concern, those choosing to pursue sociology further will become ever more cognizant of the social forces that influence our collective existence. They will see themselves not only as beneficiaries or victims of society, but also as creators—people shaping the world for current and future generations. The buyer should beware, because developing a sociological imagination undermines the relaxing comfort of being able to take social connections for granted. It reminds us to think of ourselves in relation to others and to consider the types of responsibilities we share in our interconnected world. This is the danger, as well as the promise, of the sociological imagination.

REFERENCE

Berger, Peter. 1963. *Invitation to Sociology: A Humanist Perspective.* Garden City, NY: Doubleday.

INDEX